A

HANDBOOK

FOR

MULTICULTURAL STUDIES

IN

ELEMENTARY SCHOOLS

BOOK I

CHICANO

BLACK

ASIAN

AND

NATIVE AMERICANS

ROSELLA LINSKIE

HOWARD ROSENBERG

1978

II

TO ALL OF OUR STUDENTS EVERYWHERE WHO HAVE
SO GENEROUSLY ENRICHED OUR RICE BOWL.

ISBN 88247-494-4

COPYRIGHT 1978 BY
ROSELLA LINSKIE AND HOWARD ROSENBERG

LIBRARY OF CONGRESS CARD CATALOG NUMBER:
77-91289

PUBLISHERS
ROBERT D. REED AND ADAM S. ETEROVICH

PUBLISHED BY
R & E RESEARCH ASSOCIATES, INCORPORATED
4843 MISSION STREET
SAN FRANCISCO, CALIFORNIA 94112

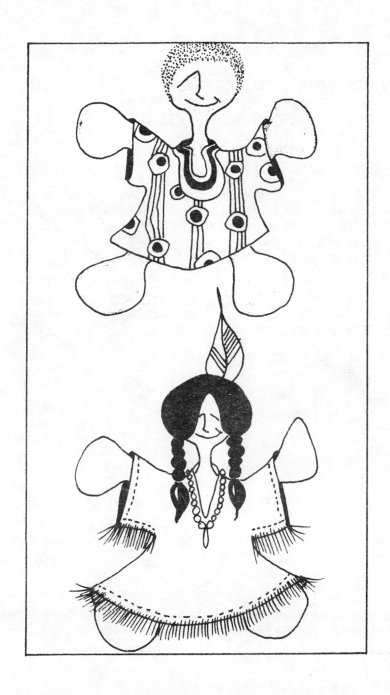

TABLE OF CONTENTS

PREFACE

THERE IS A BEAUTIFUL CHINESE TOAST
USUALLY OFFERED AT WEDDINGS, THE OPENINGS
OF BUSINESSES, OR AT THE CEREMONIAL
BEGINNINGS OF ANY NEW VENTURES. IT SAYS
..... MAY YOU ALWAYS HAVE RICE FOR YOUR
BOWL AND FRIENDS WITH WHOM TO SHARE IT!

IT IS IN THIS SPIRIT THAT WE OFFER THIS
SMALL VOLUME OF SUGGESTIONS FOR THE
ELEMENTARY SCHOOL TEACHER. THINK OF IT,
PLEASE, AS A BOWL OF IDEAS WHICH WILL
ALWAYS NEED YOUR OWN REPLENISHING AND
WHICH WILL BECOME MORE VALUABLE AND
RICHER FOR YOUR HAVING SHARED IT WITH
OTHERS.

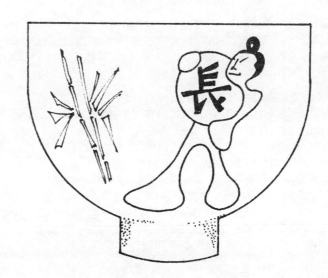

TO THE TEACHER

AFTER TWO HUNDRED YEARS, THE PEOPLE OF
THE UNITED STATES SEEM FINALLY TO HAVE
COME OF AGE SUFFICIENTLY TO MOVE OUT OF
THE ATTITUDE OF FEARING THAT WHICH IS
DIFFERENT TO THE REALIZATION OF THE VALUE
OF THE RICH MOSAIC OF CULTURAL HERITAGES
WHICH IS SO DISTINCTLY AMERICAN.

THE NATIVE AMERICANS, THE ASIANS, THE
AUSTRALIANS, THE BLACKS, THE CHICANOS,
THE EUROPEANS, THE FILIPINOS, THE SOUTH
AMERICANS, AND THE NEW ZEALANDERS - ALL
HAVE CONTRIBUTED THEIR OWN COLORFUL BITS
TO THE VARIED TAPESTRY OF THE UNITED
STATES. TRUE, LIKE ALL TAPESTRIES, THERE
ARE KNOTS, FAULTS, AND SEAMY SIDES, BUT,
TAKEN AS A WHOLE, THE UNITED STATES IS
THE WORLD'S FIRST AND MOST SUCCESSFUL
EFFORT AT BROTHERHOOD AND ONENESS.

THE SUGGESTIONS OFFERED HERE ARE IDEAS
AND ACTIVITIES THAT HAVE BEEN SUCCESSFUL
IN A VARIETY OF CLASSROOMS IN A DOZEN
DIFFERENT GEOGRAPHIC AREAS.

THE UNDERLYING ORGANIZING IDEA IS
INTEGRATION OF THE CONCEPT OF MULTI-
ETHNICITY WITH ALL THE AREAS OF THE
CURRICULUM. THERE IS CERTAINLY NO SUCH
THING AS CHICANO ARITHMETIC .....
HOWEVER, THERE ARE ARITHMETIC PROBLEMS,
COMPUTATIONS, AND CONCEPTS WHICH CAN BE
SPECIFICALLY RELATED TO A CHICANO WAY OF
LIFE AND SET OF VALUES. SO IT IS WITH
ALL AREAS OF THE CURRICULUM. THEY
DERIVE THEIR CONTENT FROM THE FOUR
CORNERS OF THE WORLD AND MUST BE WOVEN

INTO THE FABRIC OF DAILY LIVING AND
LEARNING THROUGH SKILLS AND ATTITUDE
DEVELOPMENT. THESE CAN ONLY GROW HAPPY,
HEALTHY, AND VIGOROUS IN AN ATMOSPHERE
OF TRUE ACCEPTANCE AND LOVING AWARENESS
OF THE WORTH OF EACH INDIVIDUAL CHILD,
REGARDLESS OF RACE, COLOR, CREED, OR
ECONOMIC CONDITION.

TRY THESE BITS OF INTELLECTUAL RICE FROM
OUR BOWL, BUT TRY NOT TO FORGET THAT YOU
MUST REFILL THE BOWL AS OFTEN AS POSSIBLE.

HOW TO USE THIS BOOK

EACH PAGE WILL DESCRIBE A SPECIFIC
LEARNING ACTIVITY. FOLLOWING EACH OF
THESE ACTIVITIES ARE NOTES FOR THE
TEACHER. INCLUDED ARE OUR SUGGESTED
GRADE LEVEL(S) WITH WHICH THE ACTIVITY
MIGHT BEST BE USED ..... HOWEVER .....
YOU KNOW YOUR STUDENTS AND WE ASK YOU
TO REMEMBER THAT THESE ARE SUGGESTIONS,
ONLY! AT THE END OF EACH ACTIVITY WE
HAVE PROVIDED SPACE FOR YOU TO NOTE
ACTIVITIES WHICH YOU HAVE, YOURSELF,
INVENTED, ADAPTED, OR DISCOVERED; OR
WAYS IN WHICH YOU HAVE MODIFIED OUR
SUGGESTIONS.

IT IS IMPERATIVE THAT YOU CONSIDER OUR
IDEAS AS "STARTERS." THE REAL VALUE OF
THIS BOOK IS TO HELP YOU AND YOUR
STUDENTS TO GENERATE IDEAS AND TO DESIGN
YOUR OWN MULTICULTURAL CURRICULUM.

LIFE IS A GREAT ADVENTURE. NO MORE
EXCITING A TIME EXISTS THAN THAT TIME
WHEN WE SHARE A LITTLE BIT OF OURSELVES
WITH OTHERS. WE EACH GROW A LITTLE
RICHER FOR THE EXPERIENCE.

HAPPY TEACHING!

I AM ME!

THIS ACTIVITY EMPHASIZES THE IMPORTANCE OF EACH CHILD'S SELF-CONCEPT, WITH PARTICULAR ATTENTION TO HIS ACTUAL PHYSICAL APPEARANCE. AS HE BECOMES INCREASINGLY AWARE OF HIMSELF IN RELATIONSHIP TO OTHERS, HE WILL COME TO RECOGNIZE THE UNIQUE FACTORS WHICH DISTINGUISH HIM FROM EVERYONE ELSE IN THE WORLD.

SUGGESTED GRADE LEVEL: PRIMARY

MATERIALS NEEDED:

1. A FULL-LENGTH MIRROR
2. AN INSTANT COPY CAMERA
3. LARGE SHEETS OF BUTCHER PAPER (AT LEAST 24X36")
4. NEWSPAPERS (WHICH MAY BE TAPED END-TO-END TO FORM LONG SHEETS)
5. LARGE WAX CRAYONS (UNWRAPPED)
6. TEMPERA PAINT (ASSORTED COLORS)
7. EASEL BRUSHES
8. FELT TIP MARKERS (BLACK BROAD TIP AND ASSORTED COLORS)
9. SCISSORS
10. STRING

ACTIVITIES:

1. ENCOURAGE CHILD TO STAND IN FRONT OF MIRROR AND REALLY LOOK AT HIMSELF. HAVE HIM WALK UP CLOSE TO THE GLASS AND THEN, SLOWLY, BACK AWAY, ALL THE WHILE WATCHING HIMSELF (IMAGE.) ENCOURAGE HIM TO MAKE FACES, POSE IN FUNNY POSITIONS, BEND OVER, HOP UP AND DOWN, TURN HIS BACK TO THE MIRROR AND TRY TO SEE HIMSELF OVER HIS SHOULDER, AND ANY OTHER THINGS WHICH WILL ALLOW HIM TO CONFRONT HIS IMAGE AND COME TO KNOW WHAT HE REALLY LOOKS LIKE.

2. AFTER EACH CHILD HAS HAD A CHANCE TO CONFRONT HIS OWN IMAGE, HIS OWN RE-FLECTION ALONE, ENCOURAGE TWO OR MORE TO CONFRONT THEMSELVES, TOGETHER, IN THE GLASS; ENCOURAGING THEM TO REC-OGNIZE THE DIFFERENCES BETWEEN THEM AS WELL AS THE SIMILARITIES, (DAVID'S TALLER THAN ME BUT MY HAIR IS BLONDER AND MY ARMS ARE LONGER, ETC.)

3. TAKE INDIVIDUAL PHOTOGRAPHS OF EACH CHILD AND BEGIN A WALL OF IMAGES IN "OUR ROOM" DRAWING THE PARALLEL BE-TWEEN EACH CHILD'S FAMILY AT "HOME" AND "OUR FAMILY IN SCHOOL."

4. STIMULATE DISCUSSION AMONG THE CHILDREN WHICH WILL ALLOW THEM TO VERBALIZE LIKENESSES AND DIFFERENCES AND SEE IF THEY ARE ABLE TO ACCOUNT FOR THEM.

5. ON LARGE SHEETS OF PAPER (BUTCHER PAPER IF POSSIBLE; IF NOT, NEWSPAPER WILL DO) HAVE EACH CHILD LIE DOWN AND HAVE A PARTNER DRAW HIS OUTLINE ON THE PAPER.

6. IF BUTCHER PAPER IS USED, CRAYONS AND/OR TEMPERA MAY BE USED TO COLOR THE RESULTING FORM. THEN CUT OUT THE FORM AND HANG IT BY A STRING.

7. IF YOU HAVE THE FORMS CUT OUT YOU MIGHT CARRY THE LESSON FURTHER BY HAVING THE BACK OF THE FORM FILLED IN AS THE PERSON'S BACK LOOKS. THIS IS A GREAT HELP IN BUILDING THE CONCEPT

OF "FRONT AND BACK."

8. IF BUTCHER PAPER IS UNAVAILABLE NEWSPAPER MAY BE SUBSTITUTED BUT THE CHILD'S OUTLINE SHOULD BE DONE WITH HEAVY FELT TIP MARKER AND/OR TEMPERA PAINT.

9. ALLOW THE CHILDREN TO DECIDE WHERE EACH OF THESE "PICTURES OF ME" IS GOING TO HANG IN THE CLASSROOM.

NOTES FOR THE TEACHER

THE SELF-CONCEPT OF THE CHILD IS VITAL! IT IS HOW HE DETERMINES WHETHER OR NOT HE IS "WORTH" ANYTHING, YET IT IS AN AREA WHICH IS TOO OFTEN NEGLECTED IN THE CHILD'S DEVELOPMENT.

IN THIS ACTIVITY THE TEACHER CAN HELP EACH CHILD TO RECOGNIZE IN HIMSELF SOME ONE THING WHICH MAKES HIM UNIQUE, VALUABLE, AND WORTH CAREEING ABOUT.

WHEN DISCUSSING LIKENESSES AND DIFFERENCES THE TEACHER SHOULD BE PREPARED TO DEAL WITH THE "FAIRY TALE" EXPLANATIONS AS WELL AS MORE BRUTAL AND FRANK VERSIONS. SUCH DISCUSSIONS CAN BE INVALUABLE IN AIDING THE TEACHER TO DISCOVER WHERE THE CHILDREN ARE, AND HOW THEY VIEW REALITY.

IN MULTICULTURAL EDUCATION IT IS ESSENTIAL TO RECOGNIZE THAT THE SEEDS OF INTOLER-ANCE ARE SEWN WITH THE DISREGARD FOR THE INDIVIDUAL, FIRST FOR HIMSELF, LATER FOR OTHERS. ANYTHING WHICH WILL HELP THE CHILD TO DEVELOP AN AWARENESS OF SELF, OF HIS OWN PARTICULAR WORTH, AND OF THE WORTH OF OTHERS CANNOT HELP BUT MAKE THE INDIVIDUAL A STRONGER, HEALTHIER, AND MORE OPEN PERSON.

HERE I AM! WHERE ARE YOU?

THIS ACTIVITY IS DESIGNED TO ENCOURAGE WRITING, AN IMPROVED SELF CONCEPT, AND EXPERIENCE IN CERTAIN SCIENCE CONCEPTS. IN ADDITION IT PROVIDES FEEDBACK FROM UNEXPECTED SOURCES IN THE NATURE OF RETURN MAIL.

SUGGESTED GRADE LEVEL: INTERMEDIATE

MATERIALS NEEDED:

1. A BOTTLE OF HELIUM GAS (COMPLETELY SAFE FOR USE WITH CHILDREN)
2. ONE BALLOON FOR EACH CHILD (ASSORTED COLORS)
3. ONE SAFETY PIN FOR EACH CHILD
4. ONE PREPARED INDEX CARD* FOR EACH CHILD
5. ONE FOOT OF STRING FOR EACH CHILD
6. ONE SMALL PLASTIC "BAGGIE" FOR EACH CHILD
7. A STAPLE MACHINE
8. A HOLE PUNCH

ACTIVITIES:

1. PREPARE AN UNLINED INDEX CARD (3X5") AS INDICATED* FOR EACH CHILD
2. HAVE THE YOUNGSTERS FILL IN THEIR CARD WITH AS MUCH INFORMATION AS POSSIBLE, ESPECIALLY WITH REGARD TO FAMILY, SEVERAL LIKES AND DISLIKES, FRIENDS, EVEN A PHOTOGRAPH IF THEY HAVE ONE AND WOULD LIKE TO USE IT. BOTH SIDES OF THE CARD MAY BE USED, OR EVEN A FOLDED LETTER, IF THEY REQUIRE THE SPACE.
3. THE CARD IS COMPLETED AND THEN PLACED INSIDE THE SMALL PLASTIC "BAGGIE" AND EITHER STAPLED OR TAPED CLOSED.
4. PUNCH A HOLE IN ONE CORNER OF THE "BAGGIE" BIG ENOUGH SO THAT A LENGTH OF STRING MAY BE THREADED THROUGH IT
5. THE CHILD CHOOSES A BALLOON AND FILLS IT WITH HELIUM AND TIES IT CLOSED VERY TIGHTLY
6. THE BALLOON IS THEN ATTACHED TO HIS "MESSAGE" AND IS READY FOR LAUNCHING
7. GATHER ALL OF THE YOUNGSTERS INTO A BIG CIRCLE ON THE PLAYGROUND OR IN SOME GOOD SIZED OPEN SPACE
8. MAKE A CEREMONY, AN OCASSION, A CELE-BRATION OF THE LAUNCHING OF THEIR MESSAGES ..... PERHAPS SINGING SONGS, ETC.
9. LET THE BALLOONS WITH MESSAGES GO!

*
> I AM AN_____AMERICAN
>   (ASIAN, BLACK, ETC.)
>
> I'M IN THE_____GRADE AT THE
> _____SCHOOL
>
> IN_____, _____, ____
>   (CITY)   (STATE)   (ZIP)
>
> PLEASE WRITE TO ME IF YOU FIND MY BALLOON. (INFORMATION ABOUT YOURSELF)
> _____
> _____

NOTES FOR THE TEACHER

THERE IS SIMPLY NO LIMIT IN WAYS THIS ACTIVITY MAY DEVELOP. IT MIGHT BE THE BASIS FOR A STUDY OF WEATHER, WIND CURRENTS, DISTANCES, TIME-SPACE CONCEPT FACTORS, MESSAGE TRANSMISSION AND MAIL FROM THE BEGINNING OF TIME, ETC. THE YOUNGSTERS GENERATE SUCH ENTHUSIASM AND EXCITEMENT AS THEY WAIT FOR RESPONSES AND WHEN A PIECE OF MAIL DOES, INDEED, ARRIVE FROM SOME UNKNOWN PEN-PAL WHO HAPPENS TO FIND THEIR BALLOON ..... THERE IS NOTHING LIKE IT!

A MAP MIGHT BE ESTABLISHED WITH PINS TO INDICATE WHERE THE RESPONSES ARE COMING FROM AND THIS MIGHT BE COMPARED WITH THE PREVAILING WIND FACTOR OF THE DAY WHEN THE MESSAGES WERE LAUNCHED. THIS COULD EASILY BE VERIFIED WITH THE WEATHER BUREAU. IF YOUR YOUNGSTERS SHOULD BE EARLY PRIMARY LEVEL YOU MIGHT TREAT THE ACTIVITY AS AN ADVENTURE WITH CONCEPT DEVELOPMENT APPROPRIATE TO THE LEVEL; IF THE YOUNGSTERS ARE OLDER, THERE IS NO LIMIT TO THE PHYSICAL SCIENCE POSSIBIL- ITIES WHICH CAN BE INVESTIGATED.

WHATEVER THE LEVEL, HOWEVER MUCH ACTUAL "TEACHING" IS ACCOMPLISHED WITH THIS ACTIVITY, YOU WILL BE AMAZED AND GRAT- IFIED AT THE PERSONAL ENTHUSIASM IT GENERATES.

THE TIME OF MY LIFE

THE PURPOSE OF THIS ACTIVITY IS TO HELP CHILDREN IDENTIFY, IN THEIR OWN LIVES, THE CONCEPTS OF BEFORE AND AFTER, SEQUENCE AND CONSEQUENCE, AND PAST, PRESENT, AND FUTURE.

SUGGESTED GRADE LEVEL: PRIMARY
                             INTERMEDIATE
                             ADVANCED

MATERIALS NEEDED:

1. A STRIP OF WIDE ADDING MACHINE TAPE OR A PIECE OF NEWSPRINT OR DRAWING PAPER CUT APPROXIMATELY 5" OR 6" WIDE AND EXTENDED AS LONG AS NECESSARY.
2. FELT TIP MARKERS (ASSORTED SIZE NIBS AND ASSORTED COLORS)
3. SCISSORS
4. WHITE GLUE OR RUBBER CEMENT
5. AN ASSORTMENT OF MAGAZINES FROM WHICH PHOTOGRAPHS AND/OR PICTURES MAY BE CUT

ACTIVITIES:

1. EXPLAIN TO THE YOUNGSTERS THE CONCEPT OF MAKING A VISUAL REPRESENTATION OF A PERSON'S LIFE ..... THE TIME LINE
2. ENCOURAGE EACH CHILD TO BEGIN HIS OWN TIME LINE WITH HIS OWN DATE AND PLACE OF BIRTH
3. BRING THE CHILD THROUGH THE EVENTS IN HIS LIFE WHICH SEEM IMPORTANT TO HIM BY LISTING THEM ON A PIECE OF PAPER DEVELOPING THE IDEA OF CHRONOLOGY BY FIXING AND REINFORCING THE CONCEPTS OF BEFORE AND AFTER.
4. HELP THE CHILD TO TRANSFER THE DATA FROM THE CHRONOLOGICAL LIST TO THE TIME LINE AND ENCOURAGE HIM TO PLACE THE EVENTS IN SUCH A WAY AS TO SUGGEST THE AMOUNT OF LAPSED TIME BETWEEN EVENTS IN RELATION TO ONE ANOTHER.
5. ENCOURAGE THE CHILD TO RECOGNIZE THE OPEN ENDEDNESS OF HIS TIME LINE AND THROUGH TRANSFER, THE OPEN ENDEDNESS OF HIS LIFE
6. AS HE IDENTIFIES EVENTS, ENCOURAGE HIM TO SEARCH THROUGH MAGAZINES FOR SUITABLE ILLUSTRATIONS OF SUCH EVENTS AND SHOULD SUCH MATERIAL BE UNAVAILABLE, ENCOURAGE HIM TO DRAW HIS OWN ILLUSTRATIONS.
7. ENCOURAGE THE USE OF WORDS SUCH AS BEFORE, AFTER, NEXT, THEN, BECAUSE, ETC.

6

| 1970 | 1973 | | 1976 | 1977 | 1978 |

I WAS BORN IN DALLAS TEXAS

MY NEW BABY BROTHER WAS BORN IN DALLAS TEXAS

I STARTED TO SCHOOL

I GOT THE MEASLES

WE MOVED BECAUSE MY DAD GOT A NEW JOB

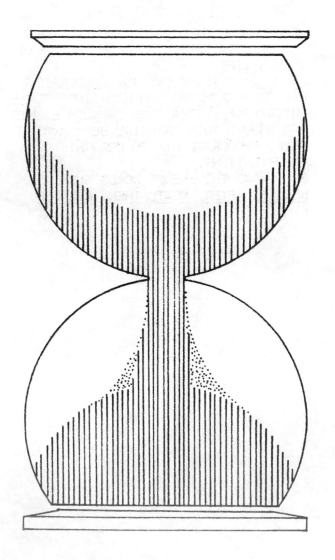

NOTES FOR THE TEACHER

THIS ACTIVITY CAN GO ON FOR AS LONG AS THERE IS MEANINGFUL LEARNING. IT CAN ALSO BE USED AS AN INTRODUCTION TO THE CONCEPT OF SIMULTANEOUS ACTION BY COMPARING LIVES AND ENCOURAGING CONCEPTS SUCH AS, "WHEN I WAS LIVING IN _____, JOHNNY WAS LIVING IN _____.

FOR MORE ADVANCED YOUNGSTERS THIS ACTIVITY CAN ALSO SERVE AS AN INTRODUCTION TO GENEALOGY. FOR EXAMPLE, "HOW LONG AGO WAS MY FATHER BORN? WHERE?" ETC.

IT CAN ALSO SERVE AS A VIVID INTRODUCTION TO THE STUDY OF HISTORY. COUNTRIES, STATES, TOWNS, AND SCHOOLS ALL HAVE THEIR OWN TIME LINES ..... THIS IS HISTORY!

FOR THE VERY YOUNG, THE PRESENT IS ALL THAT REALLY MATTERS. AS THE CHILD GROWS OLDER HE BECOMES SOMEWHAT MORE AWARE OF THE FUTURE. IT'S UNUSUAL THAT A CHILD BEFORE REACHING THE AGE OF NINE OR TEN IS ABLE TO FULLY COMPREHEND THE MEANING OF TIME PASSED AND ITS EFFECTS UPON EACH OF US.

THIS IS AN ACTIVITY WHICH CAN BE READILY ADAPTED TO ANY AGE OR GRADE LEVEL.

LET'S MAKE AN ABACUS

THIS PROJECT REQUIRES SOME FINE MOTOR SKILLS AS WELL AS IMAGINATION IN CHOOSING MATERIALS AND ASSEMBLING THE FINAL PRODUCT. IT ALSO OFFERS BOTH YOUNGSTERS AND TEACHER AN OPPORTUNITY TO EXPERIMENT WITH MATHE- MATICAL CONCEPTS AND CALCULATIONS ON A "COMPUTER" ALMOST AS OLD AS TIME ITSELF.

SUGGESTED GRADE LEVEL: INTERMEDIATE
                       ADVANCED

MATERIALS NEEDED (FOR EACH ABACUS:)

1. FOUR STYROFOAM STRIPS (2 @ 12" AND 2 @ 18")
2. FOUR UPHOLSTERY PINS
3. WHITE GLUE (CRAZY GLUE SEEMS TO WORK BEST)
4. NINE THIN BAMBOO STICKS (12" LONG SKEWERS)
5. SIXTY-THREE WOODEN OR GLASS BEADS WITH HOLES
6. ONE EXTRA PIECE OF STYROFOAM OR A HEAVIER BAMBOO ROD FOR USE AS A DIVIDER

ACTIVITIES:

1. CONSTRUCT A RECTANGULAR FRAME USING THE FOUR STYROFOAM STRIPS BY PLACING A DOB OF GLUE AT EACH JUNCTION AND INSERTING THE UPHOLSTERY PINS TO HOLD THE JOINTS
2. STRING SEVEN BEADS ON EACH OF THE NINE BAMBOO STICKS
3. FASTEN THE BAMBOO STICKS INTO THE STYROFOAM FRAME BY PUSHING EACH END SECURELY INTO THE FRAME.

4. PUSH TWO BEADS ON EACH STICK UP TO THE TOP OF THE FRAME AND THE REMAINING FIVE DOWN TO THE BOTTOM
5. IN BETWEEN, MAKE A DIVIDER USING A HEAVIER BAMBOO ROD OR ANOTHER PIECE OF STYROFOAM
6. NOW YOU SHOULD HAVE SOMETHING WHICH LOOKS LIKE THIS:

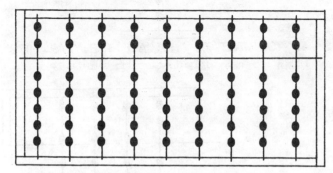

7. BY MOVING THE BEADS UP OR DOWN, YOU CAN LEARN TO ADD OR SUBTRACT OR BOTH. FOR EXAMPLE, BEADS IN THIS POSITION MEAN THE SUM IS TEN/10

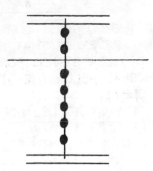

BEADS IN THIS POSITION MEAN THE SUM IS
<u>ELEVEN</u>/11

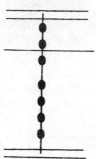

8. IF YOU WANT TO INDICATE THE YEAR 1978
    HERE IS HOW TO PLACE THE BEADS:

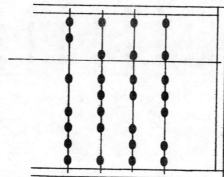

READ THE NUMBERS CLOSEST TO THE DIV-
IDER. REMEMBER THAT EACH BEAD <u>ABOVE</u>
THE DIVIDER STANDS FOR <u>FIVE</u>/5, AND
EACH BEAD BELOW THE DIVIDER STANDS
FOR <u>ONE</u>/1.

9. IF YOU WANT TO USE DOLLARS AND CENTS,
    YOU'LL NEED A MARKER BETWEEN THE
    SEVENTH AND EIGHTH STICK TO REPRESENT
    THE DECIMAL POINT ..... YOU MIGHT USE
    A PAPER CLIP OR A CLOTHES PIN. FOR
    EXAMPLE, $ 4.35 MIGHT LOOK LIKE EITHER
    OF THE FOLLOWING WHEN INDICATED ON

THE ABACUS:

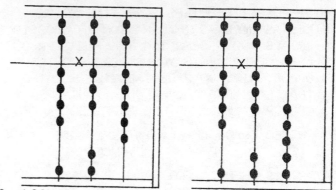

10. LOOK IN YOUR ARITHMETIC BOOK, THE DIC-
    TIONARY, OR THE ENCYCLOPOEDIA FOR
    OTHER IDEAS ABOUT THE ABACUS.

NOTES FOR THE TEACHER

THE WORD ABACUS COMES FROM THE OLD LATIN
WORD MEANING PEBBLES OR STONES. THESE
WERE USED AS COUNTERS LONG BEFORE ADDING
MACHINES AND COMPUTERS WERE INVENTED. IT
WAS RATHER CLUMSY TO HAVE TO CARRY ABOUT A
POCKET FULL OF STONES FOR CALCULATING, SO
HERE WAS A CONCEPT WAITING FOR AN INVEN-
TION. IN ABOUT THE FIFTH CENTURY BEFORE
CHRIST, THE CHINESE STARTED USING BAMBOO
STICKS AS COUNTERS AND, SOON AFTER, IT
WAS THE KOREANS WHO PUT THE TWO IDEAS
TOGETHER AND MADE THE ABACUS BY DRILLING
HOLES IN STONES AND BEADS AND STRINGING
THEM ON BAMBOO STICKS. STILL LATER, IT
WAS THE JAPANESE WHO MADE A FRAME TO HOLD
THE STICKS AND THIS WAS THE FIRST REAL
COUNTING MACHINE.

ALTHOUGH YOUR STUDENTS MAY NOT YET BE
READY FOR WORKING IN A DIFFERENT BASE
SYSTEM FROM THE DECIMAL BASE (10,) YOU
CAN MAKE A DECIMAL ABACUS AS SHOWN. BE
SURE THAT THE YOUNGSTERS UNDERSTAND THAT
THE DECIMAL IS MOVEABLE, WHICH IS WHY THE
PAPER CLIP OR CLOTHES PIN IS USEFUL.

YOU MIGHT DECIDE TO MAKE ONE VERY LARGE
ABACUS TO HANG FROM THE CEILING OF YOUR
ROOM, OR TO PUT ON THE WALL . . . . .
ADJUST THE SIZE TO FIT THE ROOM AND
YOUR NEEDS.

HINTS

MANY SMALL APPLIANCE STORES HAVE STYRO-
FOAM FRAMES OR "PACKING COLLARS" WHICH
THEY WILL GLADLY GIVE TO YOU.

BAMBOO STICKS (SKEWERS) MAY BE FOUND IN
BUNDLES OF ONE HUNDRED IN HOUSEWARE
DEPARTMENTS AND ARE USUALLY FOUND IN CLOSE
PROXIMITY TO FONDUE SETS AND SUPPLIES.

BEADS, EITHER GLASS OR WOOD, CAN BE FOUND
IN ALL KINDS OF SHOPS: DECORATOR, FABRIC,
HARDWARE, HOBBY, ETC.

TEACHER'S NOTES

WHERE IN THE WORLD DID I COME FROM?

THE PURPOSE OF THIS ACTIVITY IS TO POINT OUT TO THE YOUNGSTERS THAT IF WE TRACE BACK FAR ENOUGH WE WILL FIND THAT, EXCEPT FOR THE NATIVE AMERICANS, WE ARE ALL FOREIGNERS.

SUGGESTED GRADE LEVEL: PRIMARY
INTERMEDIATE
ADVANCED

MATERIALS NEEDED:

1. A LARGE WORLD MAP
2. A SELECTION OF COLORED YARNS (IDEALLY, A DIFFERENT COLOR FOR EACH YOUNGSTER.)
3. SCOTCH TAPE
4. THUMB TACKS
5. MAP PINS (ASSORTED COLORS)
6. AN ARTIFACT OR FAMILY HEIRLOOM (A PHOTOGRAPH, AN ARTICLE OF CLOTHING, A PIECE OF COSTUME JEWELRY, A DOLL, ETC.)

ACTIVITIES:

1. ASK EACH CHILD TO INTERVIEW HIS PARENTS AND/OR HIS GRANDPARENTS TO FIND OUT WHERE HIS FAMILY ORIGINATED.
2. AS THE INFORMATION IS COLLECTED, EACH CHILD LOCATES THE PLACE ON THE MAP WHERE HIS FAMILY ORIGINATED AND IDENTIFIES IT WITH A MAP PIN.
3. A LENGTH OF YARN IS ATTACHED TO THE ARTIFACT OR ITEM WHICH HE HAS BROUGHT WHICH RELATES TO HIS ORIGINS AND THE OTHER END OF THE LENGTH OF YARN IS SECURED TO THE MAP PIN IDENTIFYING THE PLACE OF ORIGIN.
4. IF THE YOUNGSTER IS ABLE TO FIND OUT WHERE BOTH HIS MOTHER'S AND FATHER'S FAMILIES ORIGINATED, THEN HE HAS A CHANCE TO USE TWO, THREE, OR MORE PIECES OF YARN AND TO BRING AS MANY ITEMS FOR EXHIBIT.
5. HAVE A "SHARING OUR ROOTS" DAY. ENCOURAGE EACH YOUNGSTER DESCRIBE WHAT HE BROUGHT IN AS REPRESENTATIVE OF HIS FAMILY AND WHAT HE HAS BEEN ABLE TO DISCOVER ABOUT HIS ANCESTORS.
6. INVITE PARENTS TO COME TO THE EXHIBIT. MANY OF THEM MAY HAVE A GREAT DEAL OF INTEREST IN THE GENEALOGY APPROACH AND MIGHT HAVE ESPECIALLY INTERESTING STORIES TO TELL.

NOTES FOR THE TEACHER

WE ARE A NATION OF IMMIGRANTS. ALMOST ALL OF US HAVE ANCESTORS WHO CAME TO AMERICA FROM OTHER PARTS OF THE WORLD.

THIS ACTIVITY WILL PROVIDE THE YOUNGSTERS WITH AN OPPORTUNITY TO TALK ABOUT THEIR OWN INDIVIDUAL BACKGROUND AND TO LEARN ABOUT THEIR ANCESTRY AND, HOPEFULLY, DEVELOP A PRIDE IN THEIR ANTECEDENTS AND ANCESTORS. IT ALSO DRAMATIZES THE CONCEPT THAT AMERICA IS A "NEW" NATION, MADE UP OF PEOPLE FROM ALL OVER THE WORLD.

FURTHER, IT STRESSES AN HISTORICAL INVESTIGATION METHOD WHICH IS, MORE AND MORE, BECOMING A VITAL TOOL IN RESEARCH .. ... THE ORAL HISTORY. TOO OFTEN, THE TREMENDOUS AGE DIFFERENCE BETWEEN YOUNG-STERS AND THEIR GRAND PARENTS PLACES A STRAIN ON THE RELATIONSHIP OR, AT LEAST, MAY MAKE THEIR RELATIONSHIP LESS FULL THAN IT COULD AND SHOULD BE. WHEN A YOUNGSTER DEMONSTRATES AN INTEREST, A NEED TO KNOW, ABOUT THE "FAMILY" IT INVARIABLY OPENS A WHOLE NEW WORLD IN COMMUNICATION BETWEEN THEM ..... A WILLINGNESS AND DESIRE TO SHARE ON THE GRANDPARENT'S PART AND AN AWAKENING TO THE GREAT WEALTH OF EXPER-IENCE AND LIVING THESE MARVELOUS PEOPLE HAVE DONE ON THE PART OF THE YOUNGSTERS.

THE TEACHER MUST ALSO BE PREPARED FOR THOSE YOUNGSTERS WHO, FOR ONE REASON OR ANOTHER, DO NOT HAVE ACCESS TO SUCH HISTORY ..... PERHAPS ORPHANS, YOUNGSTERS WHO ARE ADOPTED (ESPECIALLY IN THE CASE OF VIET-NAMESE, OR KOREAN WAR ORPHANS,) ETC.

IN SUCH CASES, ALL ONE CAN DO IS TO PIN APPROXIMATE ORIGINS BUT, AT ALL TIMES, BEING CAREFUL TO REINFORCE THE POSITIVE FACTORS OF THE YOUNGSTERS PRESENT EXIST-ANCE.

THIS IS AN ACTIVITY THAT CAN BE USED AT ANY GRADE LEVEL OR LEVEL OF DEVELOPMENT. THE ONLY DIFFERENTIATING FACTOR IS THE DEPTH TO WHICH THE STUDENT CAN BE TAKEN.

I'D LIKE TO BE .....

THIS ACTIVITY IS DESIGNED TO ENCOURAGE A CHILD'S IMAGINATION AND "FANTASY" TO REACT TO THE STIMULATION OF COSTUMES, PROPS, MAKE-UP, ETC. FOUND IN A "TREASURE CHEST." THE CHILD'S BEHAVIOR WILL OFTEN GIVE A REVEALING, MEANINGFUL INSIGHT INTO HIS BEING, HIS HOPES, HIS DREAMS, EVEN HIS FEARS. AT THE VERY LEAST, IT'S A WILDLY EXCITING, FUN-TIME, OF "DRESS-UP!"

SUGGESTED GRADE LEVEL: PRIMARY
                       INTERMEDIATE

MATERIALS NEEDED:

1. TREASURE CHEST (ANY OLD TRUNK, BOX, WARDROBE CHEST, ETC.)
2. A RECORD PLAYER
3. A VARIETY OF INSTRUMENTAL RECORDS TO ESTABLISH MOOD AND FEELING
4. COSTUME MATERIALS
    A. HATS
    B. WIGS
    C. DRESSES
    D. PANTS
    E. APRONS
    F. KIMONOS
    G. ANY FABRIC WHICH CAN BE DRAPED AND/OR TRANSFORMED INTO COSTUMES SUCH AS SARONGS, TOGAS, MUU MUUS, ETC.
5. PROP MATERIALS
    A. COSTUME JEWELRY
    B. SCARVES
    C. BOAS
    D. FANS
    E. SHOES
6. MAKE-UP
    A. CLOWN WHITE
    B. GREASE PAINT (ASSORTED COLORS)
    C. COSMETICS (LIPSTICK, EYE SHADOW, ETC. ((TRY FOR HYPO-ALERGENIC.))
    D. COLD CREAM (TO REMOVE "ART WORK")
7. SAFETY PINS
8. BOBBY PINS

ACTIVITIES:

IT'S DRESS-UP TIME! IT'S TIME FOR EACH CHILD TO BE SOMEONE ELSE, SOMEONE HE THINKS IT MIGHT BE FUN TO BE IF HE COULDN'T BE HIMSELF. IDEALLY THE YOUNGSTERS ARE CONFRONTED WITH THE "TREASURE CHEST" AND ITS CONTENTS AND GIVEN THE IDEA THAT THEY MAY DO ANY-THING WITH THE CONTENTS THEY WISH. ENCOURAGE THEM TO SELECT FROM THE VARIETY OF RECORDINGS ANY MUSIC THEY WISH TO PLAY AND TO CHANGE THE RECORD IF IT ISN'T WHAT THEY WANT. TRY TO GET THE IDEA ACROSS THAT THE TEACHER IS THERE TO HELP ..... BUT ONLY IF THEY NEED YOU AND THEN ONLY IF THEY ASK FOR HELP.

NOTES FOR THE TEACHER

WHAT SOUNDS LIKE A SIMPLE ACTIVITY CAN, OFTEN, BE THE MOST COMPLEX AND DIFFICULT TO CARRY OUT BECAUSE THE OBJECT OF THE LESSON IS FOR THE CHILDREN TO FUNCTION AS MUCH ON THEIR OWN AS POSSIBLE! THE TEACHER IS THERE ONLY AS RESOURCE, ONLY WHEN NEEDED. TRY TO KEEP YOURSELF OUT OF IT SO THAT CHOICE AND DECISION RESTS WITH THE YOUNGSTER, NOT INFLUENCED BY ANYTHING OTHER THAN COSTUME MATERIALS, EACH OTHER, AND, POSSIBLY, BY THE MUSIC PLAYING.

THE ACTIVITY IS PLANNED TO ENCOURAGE THE FANTASY FACTOR TO PLUG INTO WHAT NATURAL SELF-RELIANCE THE YOUNGSTER POSSESSES. AS YOU HAVE INDICATED NO "RULES," THE FEAR FACTOR SHOULD BE HELD AT A MINIMUM ONCE THE YOUNGSTER OVERCOMES WHAT NATURAL RETICENCE HE HAS. THE OUTCOME, HOPEFULLY, WILL SEE EACH YOUNGSTER "PERSONALIZING" HIS OWN COSTUME IN SUCH A WAY THAT IT IS UNIQUE AND "HIS VERY OWN!"

MOST IMPORTANT, AFTER ALL THE YOUNGSTERS HAVE ACCOMPLISHED THEIR "TRANSFORMATIONS" THEY CAN TALK ABOUT WHAT THEY HAVE DONE AND, MAYBE, EVEN WHY.

WHILE RECOGNIZING THE SELF CONCEPT AS BEING VITAL TO A WELL DEVELOPED PERSONALITY, IT IS ALSO IMPORTANT TO RECOGNIZE THE OTHER FACTORS WHICH AFFECT OUR DEVELOPMENT, SUCH AS MAGAZINES, NEWSPAPERS, PICTURE BOOKS, TELEVISION, STORIES WE ARE TOLD, ETC. WHATEVER SOURCE THE INSPIRATION COMES FROM, OFTEN THERE ARE ROLES WE ADAPT TO AUGMENT A PART OF OUR "SELVES"

WE MAY FEEL LACKING. FROM THE FOUR YEAR OLD RUNNING DOWN THE STREET WITH TOWEL FLAPPING BEHIND HIM SHOUTING, "UP, UP, AND AWAAAAYYYY!" TO THE MUCH OLDER, THOUGH STILL YOUNG, MAN IN THE "NOW COSTUME" OF JEANS, SHIRT OPEN TO THE WAIST, AND CHOKER OF HISHI BEADS; IN EACH CASE WE ARE ALL BITS AND PIECES OF OUR DREAMS.

SUCH AN ACTIVITY IS A HEAVEN-SENT OPPORTUNITY TO ALLOW IMAGINATION TO RUN FREE AND TO SHOW THAT SECRET PART OF OURSELVES WE RARELY HAVE OPPORTUNITY, OR COURAGE, TO EXPRESS.

ME AND MY SHADOW

THIS ACTIVITY IS DESIGNED TO POINT UP THE SIMILARITIES AMONG US REGARDLESS OF WHAT COLOR WE ARE, WHAT SIZE WE ARE, OR HOW WE TALK.

SUGGESTED GRADE LEVEL: PRIMARY

MATERIALS NEEDED:

1. LARGE SHEETS OF DRAWING PAPER (18X24" OR LARGER)
2. LARGE SHEETS OF NEWSPRINT PAPER (18X24" OR LARGER)
3. LARGE SHEETS OF BLACK CONSTRUCTION PAPER (18X24" OR LARGER)
4. CRAYONS
5. SCISSORS
6. MASKING TAPE
7. RUBBER CEMENT OR PASTE
8. SPOTLIGHT OR LARGE ELECTRIC TORCH (POWERFUL FLASHLIGHT)

ACTIVITIES:

1. MOUNT A LARGE PIECE OF NEWSPRINT PAPER ON THE WALL, USING MASKING TAPE TO ANCHOR IT AT EACH CORNER
2. PLACE A YOUNGSTER APPROXIMATELY EIGHT INCHES FROM THE PAPER (PROFILE IS THE MOST EFFECTIVE TO START) AND OBSERVE THE NATURAL SHADOW THUS CREATED
3. INTENSIFY THE SHADOW BY FOCUSING A STRONG LIGHT ON THE YOUNGSTER AND HAVE A PARTNER CAREFULLY LINE THE SILHOUETTE (IN THE INTERESTS OF AESTHETIC COMPOSITION EXTEND THE SILHOUETTE TO INCLUDE THE SHOULDER)
4. REMOVE THE NEWSPRINT PAPER FROM THE WALL AND CUT OUT THE SILHOUETTE
5. REPEAT THE PROCEDURE FOR EACH CHILD, ALLOWING EACH TO DETERMINE HIS OWN POSE
6. HAVE EACH CHILD DECIDE WHETHER HE PREFERS A WHITE SILHOUETTE MOUNTED ON A BLACK BACKGROUND OR A BLACK SILHOU-ETTE MOUNTED ON A WHITE BACKGROUND
7. USING THE NEWSPRINT CUT-OUT (CARTOON) EACH YOUNGSTER RECUTS A SILHOUETTE OUT OF THE HEAVIER WHITE DRAWING OR BLACK CONSTRUCTION PAPER
8. MOUNT THE SILHOUETTE ON CONTRASTING PAPER
9. THE SAME TECHNIQUE MAY BE USED WITH THREE, FOUR, OR MORE YOUNGSTERS SEATED SIDE BY SIDE WITH THE SHADOW OF THE GROUP REFLECTED ON PAPER AND A COM-POSITE GROUP PICTURE FORMED
10. HANDS, FEET, COMBINATIONS, ETC. MAY BE USED TO CREATE NEW, DIFFERENT, END-LESSLY INNOVATIVE COMBINATIONS; AS WELL AS COMPOSITES USING THE HEAD OF ONE CHILD, UPPER TORSO OF ANOTHER, LOWER TORSO OF ANOTHER, LEGS OF ANOTHER, FEET OF STILL ANOTHER, ETC. ETC. ETC.

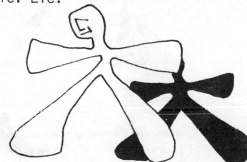

16

NOTES FOR THE TEACHER

ONE OF THE MOST DIFFICULT CONCEPTS FOR A
CHILD TO COMPREHEND IS THAT EACH OF US
LOOKS SO DIFFERENT, YET WE ARE ALL
CONSTRUCTED OF THE SAME NUMBER OF PARTS,
BASICALLY LOCATED IN THE SAME PLACES. IN
ACTUALITY ROBERT REDFORD AND FRANKENSTEIN
ARE COMPOSED OF THE SAME PARTS, EACH IS
JUST GROUPED DIFFERENTLY ..... AND THE
GROUPING IS WHAT SIGNALS THE DIFFERENCE!

THIS ACTIVITY IS DESIGNED TO POINT OUT THAT
NO MATTER WHAT WE MAY LOOK LIKE, WHAT COLOR
WE MAY BE, WHAT COLOR OUR HAIR AND EYES ARE,
OUR SHADOWS ARE ALL THE SAME ..... ONLY THE
CONFIGURATIONS CHANGE, AND WITHIN THOSE
CONFIGURATIONS THERE CAN BE A GREAT DEAL OF
FUN CREATING MARVELOUSLY INVENTIVE
COMPOSITIONS.

A HAT, ANY HAT, CAN CHANGE ME

THE MAGIC OF A HAT IS TOTALLY PHENOMENAL!
A FIREMAN'S HAT, A POLICEMAN'S HAT, A
SOLDIER'S HELMET, A COWBOY'S HAT, ANY HAT
CAN TURN A YOUNGSTER INTO WHATEVER HE MAY
WANT TO BE. WHEN ENCOURAGED TO MAKE HIS
OWN HAT, WHEN HE BECOMES A "MAD HATTER,"
THERE ARE NO ENDS TO THE POSSIBILITIES.
THE ESSENCE OF THIS ACTIVITY IS IN THE
MANIPULATION OF MATERIALS TO CREATE A
"HEAD COVERING" WHICH WILL CHANGE THE
YOUNGSTER. PERHAPS IT WILL BE A FANTASTIC
RELEASE OF ALL INHIBITIONS, OR SIMPLY A
WONDERFULLY ENJOYABLE FANTASY TIME.

SUGGESTED GRADE LEVEL: PRIMARY
                        INTERMEDIATE
                        ADVANCED

MATERIALS NEEDED:

1. CONSTRUCTION PAPER (9X12", 12X18" AND
    18X24" - ASSORTED COLORS)
2. TISSUE PAPER (ASSORTED COLORS
3. STAPLE MACHINES
4. PAPER CLIPS (IN ADDITION TO THE TRAD-
    ITIONAL TYPE THERE ARE OTHERS WHICH
    MIGHT SERVE A DECORATIVE PURPOSE)
5. BRAD FASTENERS
6. WHITE GLUE
7. RUBBER CEMENT
8. STRING
9. YARNS (ASSORTED WEIGHTS AND COLORS)
10. GLITTER
11. BEADS
12. SCOTCH TAPE

ACTIVITIES:

1. AFTER DEMONSTRATING SOME OF THE BASIC
    PAPER SCULPTURE TECHNIQUES SUCH AS
    BENDING, CURLING, CUTTING, FOLDING,
    FRINGING, PINKING, PLEATING, ROLLING,
    SCORING, SPLITTING, TWISTING, WEAVING,
    ETC. DEMONSTRATE SOME BASIC FORM
    APPROACHES:
    A. FASTEN ONE PIECE OF COLORED PAPER
        INTO A CYLINDER WHICH WILL FIT THE
        HEAD, USING THAT AS A BASE FOR THE
        HAT
    B. FASTEN OPPOSITE ENDS (CORNERS) OF A
        PIECE OF COLORED PAPER INTO A FORM
        WHICH WILL FIT THE HEAD, LEAVING
        ONE CORNER EXTENDED UP AND ANOTHER
        DOWN, THIS LATTER CAN BE FOLDED OR
        CURLED ALLOWING FOR FRINGING,
        PLEATING, ETC.
    C. ON A LARGE SHEET OF PAPER MAKE A
        CIRCLE HAVING AT LEAST A TWELVE
        INCH RADIUS AND CUT IT OUT. CUT A
        SLIT FROM THE OUTSIDE OF THE CIRCLE
        TO ITS CENTER, AFTER WHICH ONE EDGE
        OF THE SLIT IS OVERLAPPED SLIGHTLY
        OVER THE OTHER FORMING A CONE SHAPE
        (THE MORE OVERLAP, THE MORE PRO-
        NOUNCED THE CONE)
    D. FROM ONE PIECE OF PAPER A CIRCLE
        THE SIZE OF THE HEAD IS CUT AND THE
        CIRCLE ITSELF IS PUT ASIDE, RETAIN-
        ING THE PAPER AROUND THE CIRCLE
        WHICH IS THEN PLACED ON THE HEAD
        TO FORM AN OPEN CROWN EFFECT WHICH
        ALLOWS THE BRIM TO BECOME THE HAT.
    E. THERE ARE OTHER BASIC FORMS WHICH

THE YOUNGSTERS WILL DISCOVER FOR THEMSELVES ..... AS LONG AS THE "HAT" WILL STAY ON THE HEAD, IT'S SUCCESSFUL

2. ONCE THE BASIC FORM HAS BEEN ESTAB-LISHED, EMBELLISHMENTS CAN BE CREATED, IMPROVISED, ECCLECTISIZED, ETC.

3. TISSUE PAPER MAY BE TREATED IN MUCH THE SAME WAY AS CONSTRUCTION PAPER BUT IT MUST BE HANDLED MORE GENTLY; ALSO FASTENING IT IS SOMEWHAT MORE DIFFICULT THOUGH IT REACTS EXCEPTION-ALLY WELL TO WHITE GLUE

4. THE CHILDREN SHOULD BE ENCOURAGED TO BE AS "FAR OUT" AS THEY WISH. EACH HAT SHOULD BE A LIVING SCULPTURE WHICH EXPRESSES THE YOUNGSTER'S PERSONALITY

5. AFTER THE YOUNGSTERS HAVE MADE THEIR OWN HATS, THEY MIGHT BE SHOWN HEAD-DRESSES FROM AFRICAN, INDIAN, SOUTH AMERICAN, AND EUROPEAN AS WELL AS ORIENTAL CULTURES ..... FROM THE BE-RIBBONED, STREAMERED HATS OF THE BELGIANS TO THE CEREMONIAL MASK-HEAD-DRESSES OF THE SWAHILI AND MASAI TRIBES OF AFRICA, ETC. THIS DISPLAY OF REAL HEADDRESSES, OR OF SLIDES AND/OR PHOTOGRAPHS SHOULD BE PROVIDED ONLY AFTER THE YOUNGSTERS HAVE COMPLETED THEIR OWN

MASK HEADDRESS

COOLIE HAT

DUNCE HAT

NOTES FOR THE TEACHER

AS IN ANY ACTIVITY, IT IS THE YOUNGSTER'S INVOLVEMENT, HIS EXPERIENCE, THAT IS THE MOST VAULABLE PRODUCT. IN THIS ACTIVITY, IF THE HAT WILL REMAIN ON THE HEAD, IT IS SUCCESSFUL; BUT IT IS HOPED THAT THE EMBELLISHMENTS, THE INVENTIVE TOUCHES, THE DESIGN OF THE STRUCTURE WILL BE EXCITING, INNOVATIVE, IMAGINATIVE, COLORFUL, AND WONDERFUL FUN TO SEE.

IT IS PARTICULARLY IMPORTANT IN THIS ACTIVITY THAT VERY LITTLE STIMULATION, ESPECIALLY VISUAL, BE PROVIDED. IN THIS WAY THE PRODUCT WILL TRULY REFLECT THE YOUNGSTER'S NATIVE INTUITION AND IMAGIN- ATION. YOUR HELP SHOULD BE SUPPORTIVE IN AIDING THE YOUNGSTER TO ACCOMPLISH WHAT HE HAS, HIMSELF, SET AS GOAL(S) BUT DUE TO CERTAIN LACKS IN DEXTERITY OR MANUAL SKILL MAY BE UNABLE TO ACCOMPLISH.

THE ACTIVITY SHOULD BE INTERESTING, EXCITING, ENTERTAINING, AND FUN ..... AND WILL, IN ALL PROBABILITY, TAKE VERY LITTLE ACTUAL TIME.

PERHAPS MOST IMPORTANT IS THE TRANSFER VALUE THE ACTIVITY CARRIES WITH IT. IF COORDINATED WITH AN INTERMEDIATE LEVEL SOCIAL STUDIES LESSON, THIS ACTIVITY MIGHT BECOME AN IMPORTANT FACTOR IN COSTUME MAKING.

TEACHER'S NOTES

MAKE YOUR OWN KIND OF MUSIC

ONE OF THE MOST VITAL PARTS OF ANY CULTURE IS THE SOUND OF THAT CULTURE; THE SOUND OF THE LANGUAGE, THE SOUND OF THE PEOPLE AS THEY MOVE ABOUT, THE SOUND THAT THEIR MUSIC MAKES AS WELL AS THE WAY THAT SOUND IS MADE AND/OR PRODUCED. THIS ACTIVITY IS DESIGNED TO DEAL WITH THE SOUND(S) AND ITS PRODUCTION AND, NOT INCIDENTALLY, WITH THE COORDINATION OF SKILL FACTORS TOWARD THE PRODUCTION OF A MUSICAL INSTRUMENT.

SUGGESTED GRADE LEVEL: INTERMEDIATE
                        ADVANCED

MATERIALS NEEDED:

1. CARDBOARD ROLL (TUBE) FROM TOILET TISSUE, PAPER TOWELS, WAX PAPER, PLASTIC WRAP, ETC.
2. ELASTIC BANDS
3. STRING
4. WAX PAPER OR PLASTIC WRAP
5. SCISSORS
6. MASKING TAPE
7. SCOTCH TAPE
8. RAZOR BLADES (X-ACTO KNIVES OR MAT KNIVES IF AVAILABLE)

ACTIVITIES:

1. APROXIMATELY 1/3 OF THE WAY FROM ONE END OF THE TUBE YOU SELECT, CUT A RECTANGULAR OPENING AS INDICATED IN THE DIAGRAM, USING A RAZOR BLADE OR AN X-ACTO KNIFE OR MAT KNIFE (IF EITHER IS AVAILABLE)
2. DOUBLE A LENGTH OF PLASTIC WRAP OR WAX PAPER AND CUT A CIRCLE OF THIS

MATERIAL APPROXIMATELY ONE INCH IN DIAMETER LARGER THAN THE OPENINGS OF THE CARDBOARD TUBE AND FOLD IT OVER THE END OF THE TUBE CLOSEST TO THE RECTANGULAR OPENING
3. SECURE THE MATERIAL WITH ELASTIC BANDS AND WRAP WITH MASKING OR SCOTCH TAPE
4. WRAP THE OPPOSITE END OF THE TUBE WITH SCOTCH OR MASKING TAPE TO ACT AS THE MOUTHPIECE
5. HOLD INSTRUMENT SO THAT THE MOUTH IS PLACED AT THE OPEN END WITH THE HAND COVERING THE RECTANGULAR OPENING AND HUM INTO THE TUBE VARYING RESULTING SOUND BY CHANGING PITCH, INTENSITY, AND VOLUME
6. THE SOUND MAY ALSO BE MODIFIED BY ALLOWING RECTANGULAR OPENING TO OPEN AND CLOSE BY CHANGING POSITION OF FINGERS TO COMPLETELY BLOCK AIR OFF OR TO ALLOW AIR TO FLOW THROUGH
7. ANOTHER VARIATION IS TO DRUM FINGERS AGAINST TUBE'S SIDE OR ON THE PAPER COVERING ONE END
8. THE INSTRUMENT MAY BE FURTHER MODIFIED BY PAPIER MACHEING, PAINTING, AND DECORATING IT IN ANY NUMBER OF WAYS

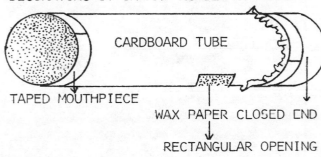

CARDBOARD TUBE

TAPED MOUTHPIECE

WAX PAPER CLOSED END

RECTANGULAR OPENING

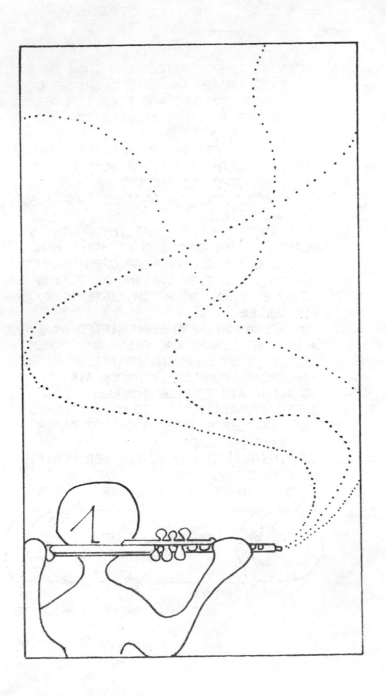

NOTES FOR THE TEACHER

THE MUSIC OF A CULTURE CONVEYS MUCH OF ITS FEELING, THE SPIRITUAL QUALITY OF ITS PEOPLE, THE "ALIVENESS" OF ITS PEOPLE. MANY TIMES THE "INSTRUMENTS" USED TO CREATE THE MUSIC ARE EXCEEDINGLY PRIMITIVE ..... ONE STICK BEING STRUCK UPON ANOTHER, OR A ROCK BEING STRUCK UPON A ROCK OF A DIFFERENT SIZE. EVEN IN THE SIMPLEST FORMS SOUND IS THE KEY FACTOR.

THE SOUND, WHEN REPEATED, STRUCTURED, OR ORDERED IN EVEN THE SIMPLEST OF PROGRES- SIONS CONVEYS A RHYTHM, A PATTERN, A "FEEL" THAT MORE SOPHISTICATED INSTRUMENTS ARE OFTEN UNABLE TO CONVEY DUE TO THEIR VERY COMPLEXITY. INHERENT IN THESE CONCEPTS IS THE IDEA OF WHAT "MUSIC" IS ALL ABOUT ..... WHEN DOES SOUND BECOME MUSIC? HOW MUCH STRUCTURE IS NECESSARY BEFORE SOUND CAN BE CALLED MUSIC? AT WHAT POINT DOES "IT" HAPPEN?

AT THE ROOT OF THE SOUND IS THE CREATION OF THE INSTRUMENT. A QUESTION THAT THEN COMES TO THE SURFACE IS ..... WHICH COMES FIRST, INSTRUMENT OR NEED TO MAKE A PARTIC- ULARE SOUND? IT'S THE OLD "FORM VERSES FUNCTION" IDEA OR, PERHAPS, IT GOES BACK EVEN FURTHER TO "WHICH CAME FIRST, THE CHICKEN OR THE EGG?"

THIS ACTIVITY IS AN ATTEMPT TO SHOW A WAY TO CREATE A SIMPLE INSTRUMENT FROM WHICH ANYONE CAN COAX A VARIETY OF SOUNDS. IT ROOTS TO THE REED AND WOODWIND INSTRUMENTS THE AFRICANS USED CENTURIES AGO.

LONG DISTANCE, PLEASE!

THIS ACTIVITY IS DESIGNED TO ENCOURAGE ORAL COMMUNICATION SKILLS, A KNOWLEDGE OF AND PRACTICE WITH TELEPHONE COURTESY, AND THE DEVELOPMENT OF TIME AND DISTANCE CONCEPTS.

IN ADDITION, THE CONVERSATIONAL SKILLS ENCOURAGED BY THIS ACTIVITY WILL, OF NECESSITY, STRENGTHEN THE GENERAL BACK-GROUND KNOWLEDGE POSSESSED BY EACH OF THE YOUNGSTERS IN ORDER THAT HE WILL BE ABLE TO RESPOND TO QUESTIONS POSED BY THE PEOPLE "CALLING!"

SUGGESTED GRADE LEVEL: PRIMARY
                                INTERMEDIATE

MATERIALS NEEDED:

1. A LARGE WALL MAP OF THE WORLD
2. TWO TELEPHONES (LOCAL TELEPHONE COMPANIES ARE USUALLY VERY HELPFUL WITH THIS KIND OF ACTIVITY, LOANING TELEPHONES AND OFFERING OTHER HELP BY WAY OF FILMS, FILMSTRIPS, ETC. WHICH MIGHT ADD IMMEASURABLY TO THE LEARNING PROCESS)
3. TWO LENGTHS OF RIBBON OR STRING

ACTIVITIES:

1. ENCOURAGE EACH YOUNGSTER TO SELECT THE POINT OF ORIGIN OF HIS TELEPHONE CALL (USUALLY THE YOUNGSTERS PICK A SPOT CLOSE TO HOME AS THEY BEGIN)
2. FASTEN ONE END OF A LENGTH OF RIBBON OR STRING TO THE PLACE ON THE MAP MOST CLOSELY ALLIED TO THE POINT OF ORIGIN OF THE YOUNGSTER'S CALL AND ATTACH THE OTHER END TO HIS TELEPHONE
3. ENCOURAGE THE YOUNGSTER TO SELECT THAT POINT HE WISHES TO CALL (OPEN THE CHOICE TO INCLUDE ANYWHERE IN THE WORLD
4. FASTEN ONE END OF A LENGTH OF RIBBON OR STRING TO THAT SPOT ON THE MAP AND ATTACH THE OTHER END TO THE SECOND TELEPHONE
5. PREPARE THE CHILDREN TO ANSWER QUES-TIONS ABOUT WEATHER, CLOTHING, FOOD, HOUSING, CUSTOMS, ETC. ESPECIALLY IF AND WHEN THE CALLS SHOULD DEVELOP INTO OVERSEAS CALLS
6. ALLOW THE CHILDREN TO TAKE TURNS CARRYING ON LONG DISTANCE CONVERSA-TIONS ENCOURAGING THEM TO PAY CAREFUL ATTENTION TO THE DIFFERENT TIME ZONES, STATION TO STATION AND PERSON TO PERSON RATES, WEATHER CONDITIONS, AND CLIMATE AND SEASONAL DIFFERENCES

NOTES FOR THE TEACHER

THE LEARNING POSSIBILITIES INHERENT IN THIS ACTIVITY ARE PRACTICALLY LIMITLESS DEPENDING UPON HOW THE ACTIVITY IS STRUCTURED.

WE WOULD ENCOURAGE YOU TO ENLIST THE HELP OF YOUR LOCAL TELEPHONE COMPANY WHICH IS, AFTER ALL, A COMMERCIAL ENTITY BASED ON A PROFIT MOTIVE AND CERTAINLY POSITIVELY DISPOSED TOWARD ANY ACTIVITY WHICH WILL ENCOURAGE THE USE OF THEIR PRODUCT ..... TELEPHONE SERVICES. MANY TELEPHONE SYSTEMS HAVE TRAVELING EXHIBITS WHICH DETAIL THE HISTORY OF THE TELEPHONE AND DISPLAY THE EVOLUTION OF THE INSTRUMENT EITHER IN A MEDIA PRESENTATION OR WITH ACTUAL EXAMPLES OF THE INSTRUMENTS THEM-SELVES. SUCH AN EXHIBIT IS, IN ITS WAY, A CAPSULE HISTORY OF COMMUNICATION. IN ADDITION, MOST COMPANIES ARE DELIGHTED TO LOAN INSTRUMENTS FOR SUCH ACTIVITIES AS THESE. THERE ARE ALSO OTHER AIDS WITH WHICH THE TELEPHONE COMPANY MAY PROVIDE YOUR CLASS IF YOU TAKE THE TIME AND EFFORT TO PLUMB THE POSSIBILITIES.

WHEN MAKING YOUR BASIC PLANS, INCLUDE THE DIFFERENT TYPES OF TELEPHONE CALL WITH WHICH THE YOUNGSTERS MIGHT BECOME IN-VOLVED: LOCAL CALLS, TOLL CALLS, STATION TO STATION CALLS, PERSON TO PERSON CALLS, TRANS-CONTINENTAL AND TRANS-OCEANIC CALLS. CONCERN THE YOUNGSTERS WITH OTHER QUES-TIONS AFFECTING THEIR CALLS ..... TIME ZONES (WHAT TIME WILL IT BE IN LONDON IF IT'S 11:00 A.M. HERE?) RATES (SHOULD I MAKE IT STATION TO STATION AND TAKE THE CHANCE THAT SOMEONE ELSE WILL ANSWER AND THE PERSON THAT I WANT TO REACH WON'T BE HOME? HOW MUCH MORE WILL IT COST TO CALL PERSON TO PERSON AND IS IT WORTH THE DIFFERENCE?) WEATHER CONDITIONS (IT'S WINTER IN BUENOS AIRES, WILL THAT AFFECT MY CALL?) INTERNATIONAL DATE LINE (IT'S 9:30 A.M. ON OCTOBER 29 HERE ..... WHAT TIME WILL IT BE IN TOKYO, AND WHAT DAY?)

EACH QUESTION, EACH CONSIDERATION OFFERS LIMITLESS POSSIBILITIES TO INCREASE THE YOUNGSTER'S KNOWLEDGE ABOUT THE WORLD WITH REGARD TO DATES, TIMES, CLIMATES, SEASONS, ETC. THIS IS PROBABLY ONE OF THE MOST EFFECTIVE GEOGRAPHY LESSONS POSSIBLE BUT THERE IS VIRTUALLY NO "THREAT FACTOR" PRESENT, AT ALL. WHERE A GLOBE AND A BOOK IS "SCHOOL BEHAVIOR," A TELEPHONE IS "IN-LIFE BEHAVIOR," AND FAR MORE COM-FORTABLE.

THE ACTIVITY MAY BE ENRICHED IF YOU HAVE BI-LINGUEL YOUNGSTERS IN THE CLASS AND THE USE OF ANOTHER LANGUAGE, AND A TRANSLATOR IS ENCOURAGED. WHILE SOME YOUNGSTERS ARE MAKING THEIR TELEPHONE CALLS, OTHER MAY BE ACTING AS "OPERATORS," WHILE OTHERS MAY BE COMPUTING CHARGES, ETC.

THE USES OF SCIENCE, MATHEMATICS, LOGIC, ETHICS, AND SO MANY OTHER PARTS OF THE SOCIAL SCIENCES MAKE THIS A TRULY INTEG-RATED ACTIVITY.

THE RATTLE

ANY MATERIAL WHICH PRODUCES NOISE COULD, CONCEIVABLY, BECOME A MUSICAL INSTRUMENT DEPENDING UPON HOW THAT NOISE IS ORDERED AND THE VOLUME AND INTENSITY AT WHICH IT IS PITCHED. IN A RATTLE THE NOISE IS PRODUCED BY OBJECTS HITTING AGAINST ONE ANOTHER AND/OR AGAINST THE SIDES OF THE CONTAINER INTO WHICH THEY ARE PLACED. FOR EXAMPLE: A HANDFUL OF PEBBLES SHAKEN INSIDE A LOOSLY CLOSED FIST WILL PRODUCE A NOISE, BUT THAT NOISE WILL CHANGE SUBSTANTIALLY WHEN THE SAME MATERIALS ARE SHAKEN INSIDE OF A CONTAINER WHICH WILL NOT MUFFLE THE SOUND.

THIS ACTIVITY IS DESIGNED TO PROVIDE THE YOUNGSTERS WITH AN OPPORTUNITY TO CREATE A BASIC MUSICAL INSTRUMENT OR "NOISE-MAKER" WHICH WILL ALLOW EACH YOUNGSTER TO ENGAGE IN A PROJECT WHICH STIMULATES THE COORDINATION OF SMALL AND LARGE MUSCLE MOVEMENTS TOWARD THE CONSTRUCTION OF THE "INSTRUMENT" AND ENCOURAGES THE SAME FACILITY WHEN COAXING SOUND FROM THE "INSTRUMENT" ONCE IT IS PRODUCED.

SUGGESTED GRADE LEVEL: PRIMARY
                          INTERMEDIATE

MATERIALS NEEDED:

1. CARDBOARD ROLLS (TUBES) FROM TOILET TISSUES, PAPER TOWELS, WAX PAPER, ALUMINUM FOIL, PLASTIC WRAP, ETC.
2. EMPTY BOXES (SMALL) FROM CEREAL, SALT CONTAINERS, OATMEAL BOXES, ETC.
3. FLAT CARDBOARD
4. MASKING TAPE
5. NEWSPAPER
6. PAPER TOWELS (WHITE OR BUFF)
7. WALLPAPER PASTE
8. WATER AND PASTE CONTAINERS (COFFEE CANS ARE IDEAL)
9. SCISSORS
10. WHITE GLUE
11. COLORED CONSTRUCTION PAPER (9X12" ASSORTED COLORS)
12. TISSUE PAPER (ASSORTED COLORS)
13. ASSORTED DRIED VEGETABLES AND GRAINS (POPCORN ((POPPED AND UNPOPPED),) LIMA BEANS, PINTO BEANS, PEAS, BARLEY, BIRDSEED, ETC.)
14. PEBBLES
15. TEMPERA PAINT (ASSORTED COLORS)
16. FELT TIP MARKERS (ASSORTED SIZES AND COLORS)
17. EASEL BRUSHES

ACTIVITIES:

1. SHOULD THE YOUNGSTERS ELECT TO USE THE CARDBOARD ROLL (TUBE) AS A BASE .....
   A) TRACE TWO CARDBOARD ROUNDS USING THE ENDS OF THE ROLL THEY WILL USE AND CUT THEM OUT
   B) BLOCK ONE END OF THE ROLL BY PLACING ONE CARDBOARD ROUND OVER THE OPENING AND SECURING WITH TAPE
   C) PLACE WHATEVER SINGLE ITEM OR COMBINATION OF ITEMS YOU CHOOSE TO MAKE THE SOUND OF YOUR "INSTRUMENT" INSIDE THE CONTAINER
   D) BLOCK THE OTHER END OF THE ROLL BY PLACING THE OTHER CARDBOARD ROUND OVER THAT OPENING AND SECURING WITH TAPE

2. SHOULD THE YOUNGSTER ELECT TO USE THE EMPTY CEREAL BOX, SALT BOX, OR OATMEAL CONTAINER AS A BASE .....
   A) PLACE WHATEVER SINGLE ITEM OR COMBINATION OF ITEMS YOU CHOOSE TO MAKE THE SOUND OF YOUR "INSTRUMENT" INSIDE THE CONTAINER
   B) TAPE ANY OPENINGS SECURELY CLOSED TAKING CARE THAT THE "STICKY" PART OF THE TAPE CANNOT COME INTO DIRECT CONTACT WITH ANY OF THE ITEMS WHICH WILL MOVE ABOUT TO CREATE THE NOISE

3. ONE OF THE MOST IMPORTANT ASPECTS OF THIS ACTIVITY IS THE "NOISE" OR THE "MUSIC" WHICH WILL BE PRODUCED, SO WHEN THE CONTAINERS ARE FILLED, SHAKE THE RATTLE TO SEE IF THE SOUND IS WHAT YOU WANT ..... IF IT IS YOU ARE READY TO PROCEED, IF NOT, THIS IS THE TIME TO RE-OPEN THE CONTAINER AND CHANGE THE MATERIALS

4. TEAR NEWSPAPER INTO SMALL STRIPS (APPROXIMATELY 1X5") AND SET ASIDE ..... THE TEARING IS IMPORTANT SO THAT THE EDGES WILL RAG AND BIND MORE SECURELY

5. MIX UP A BATCH OF WALLPAPER PASTE ACCORDING TO THE DIRECTIONS ON THE PACKAGE (ALWAYS SPRINKLE THE POWDER OVER THE SURFACE OF THE LIQUID AND ALLOW THE LIQUID TO ABSORB THE MATERIAL ..... <u>DO NOT STIR</u> ..... UNTIL THE MIXTURE IS SUPERSATURATED AND THEN KNEAD THE MIXTURE WITH HANDS TO SMOOTH AWAY ANY LUMPS) ADDING A GENEROUS SQUEEZE OF WHITE GLUE (WHICH TENDS TO PLASTICIZE THE SOLUTION DISCOURAGING "LITTLE CREATURES" THAT LIKE PAPIER MACHE

6. USING THE TORN NEWSPAPER STRIPS, TAKE ONE AT A TIME, DIP IT INTO THE PASTE SOLUTION AND APPLY TO THE "INSTRUMENT" UNTIL YOU HAVE APPLIED ONE COMPLETE LAYER OVERLAPPING THE STRIPS IN A CRISS-CROSS FASHION

7. FOR SUCCESSIVE LAYERS, ALTERNATE ONE PIECE OF NEWSPAPER DIPPED IN THE PASTE SOLUTION WITH ONE PIECE OF DRY NEWSPAPER UNTIL YOU HAVE APPROXIMATELY FIVE LAYERS OF NEWSPAPER AND ONE LAYER OF PAPER TOWELLING (THIS LAST PROVIDES A SMOOTH, NEUTRAL COVERING WHICH IS A FINE BASE FOR ANY DECORATIVE APPLICATION)

8. ALLOW TO DRY FOR AT LEAST TWENTY-FOUR HOURS AND PERHAPS (DEPENDING UPON CLIMATE AND HUMIDITY) FORTY-EIGHT HOURS WOULD BE BETTER

9. WHEN THOROUGHLY DRY, THE MATERIALS INSIDE SHOULD "RATTLE ABOUT" AND CONVEY A VERY DEFINITE CHARACTER TO THE SOUND THE INSTRUMENT PRODUCES

10. DECORATIVE APPLICATIONS CAN BE ACCOMPLISHED IN ANY NUMBER OF WAYS .....
    A) COLORED CONSTRUCTION PAPER MAY BE BOUND AROUND THE FORM USING WHITE GLUE TO SECURE IT (STRIPES, ZIG-ZAGS, ETC. ARE NOT ONLY POSSIBLE BUT DESIREABLE
    B) TEMPERA PAINT DECORATION IN A MULTITUDE OF WAYS IS POSSIBLE
    C) OVER THE TEMPERA PAINT, CHANELS OF WHITE GLUE ADD INTERESTING AND EFFECTIVE DESIGN POSSIBILITIES
    D) YARN, RIBBONS, COLORED THREADS MAY

BE WRAPPED AROUND THE FORM AND
SECURED WITH WHITE GLUE

E) CUT-OUTS FROM MAGAZINES AND NEWS-
PAPERS ARE POSSIBLE DECORATIVE
ADDITIVES

F) TISSUE PAPER COLLAGE IS MOST
EFFECTIVE WITH THIS TYPE OF FORM
AND MAY BE ACCOMPLISHED BY MIXING
A MEDIUM WHICH IS TWO PARTS WHITE
GLUE AND ONE PART WARM WATER IN A
WELL MIXED SOLUTION AND PAINTING
THIS SOLUTION OVER THE FORM AND
PLACING TISSUE PAPER OVER THE FORM
WHILE THE SOLUTION IS STILL WET
PAINTING OVER THE TISSUE PAPER
WITH MORE OF THE SOLUTION .....
THE MILKY ADHESIVE SOLUTION DRIES
RELATIVELY CLEAR AND THE MARBLE
LIKE, TRANSLUSCENT SURFACE WHICH
RESULTS IS EXCEPTIONALLY EFFECTIVE

11. WHATEVER FORM THE DECORATION TAKES,
THIS COLLAGE MEDIUM DESCRIBED ABOVE
IS AN IDEAL "SEALER" WHICH WILL PRE-
SERVE THE FORM AND DECORATION MUCH AS
SHELLAC OR VARNISH DOES BUT WITH FAR
LESS DIFFICULTY ..... AND IT MAY BE
"PAINTED" OVER THE ENTIRE SURFACE AND
LEFT TO DRY

12. WHATEVER FORM OF DECORATION IS USED,
THE ACTIVITY MAY BE CONSIDERABLY
ENRICHED BY ENCOURAGING THE YOUNGSTERS
TO PAY CAREFUL ATTENTION TO THE FORM
AND FUNCTION OF THEIR "INSTRUMENT"
AND BASE THEIR DESIGN CONSIDERATIONS
ON SUCH POINTS

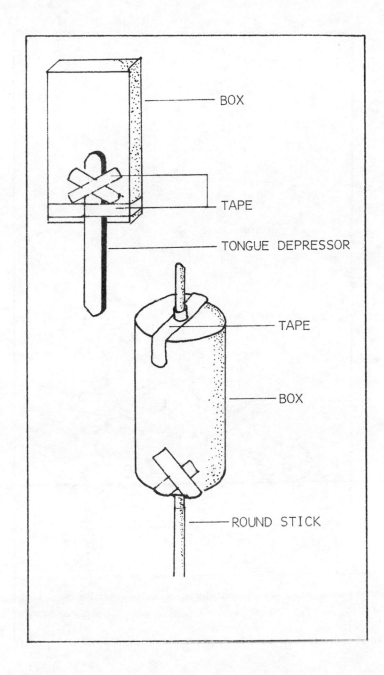

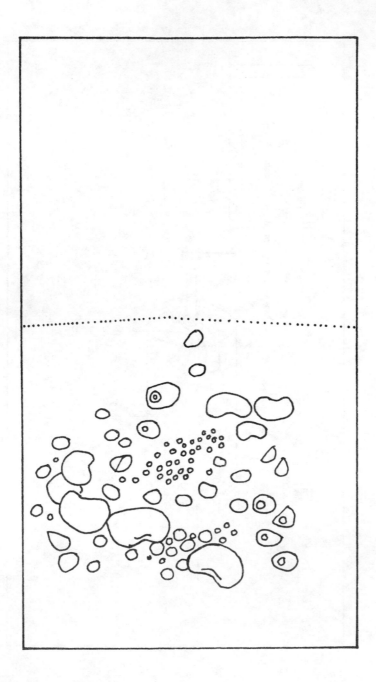

NOTES FOR THE TEACHER

AT THE OUTSET OF THIS ACTIVITY, EACH OF
THE YOUNGSTERS SHOULD HAVE THE OPPORTUNITY
TO EXPERIMENT WITH A NUMBER OF DIFFERENT
MATERIALS TO DETERMINE WHAT THE SOUNDS OF
EACH ARE ABOUT AND, POSSIBLY, TO DETERMINE
WHAT COMBINATIONS OF MATERIALS MIGHT SOUND
LIKE.

THE RATTLE IS AN "INSTRUMENT" WHICH HAS
COME DOWN THROUGH HISTORY FOR THOUSANDS OF
YEARS AND A REALLY EXCITING RESEARCH
PROJECT MIGHT INVOLVE LISTENING TO
RECORDINGS OF TRIBAL MUSIC FROM AFRICA,
MUSIC FROM SPAIN, AND MUSIC FROM MEXICO
TRYING TO "PICK OUT" THE SOUND OF THE
RATTLE IN ITS VARIOUS FORMS IN MUSIC FROM
THE VERY PRIMITIVE TO THE SOPHISTICATED UP
TO, AND INCLUDING, ROCK MUSIC PRODUCED BY
CONTEMPORARY GROUPS.

THE SOUND OF THE RATTLE WILL BE VERY MUCH
LIKE THAT OF THE MARACA ..... AND A LITTLE
RESEARCH, WHICH CAN BE DONE AT THE LIBRARY
OR THROUGH TEXTS IN YOUR OWN CLASSROOM,
WILL SHOW THAT CIVILIZATIONS AS FAR BACK
AS THE MAYAN AND AZTEC USED THIS
"INSTRUMENT." IT WOULD BE A FINE CONCEPT-
UAL LEARNING ACTIVITY TO RELATE THE REST
OF THE WORLD TO THESE CIVILIZATIONS ON A
TIME-LINE BASE.

WHEN CONSIDERING HOW "ESOTERIC" SOME
LEARNING CAN BE, IT'S RATHER EXCITING TO
THINK THAT SOMETHING AS SIMPLE AS THE
RATTLE CAN BE USED TO RETRACE MUCH OF THE
HISTORY OF MUSIC AND, BY EXTENSION,
CULTURE AND RELIGION.

MAKE YOUR OWN KIND OF MUSIC I

THE MAKING OF A MARACA IS AN EXPERIENCE WHICH REQUIRES MOTOR SKILL COORDINATION AND CREATIVITY IN DETERMINING SOUND POSSIBILITIES, DECORATIVE APPLICATIONS, AND HANDLING TEMPERA PAINT, OIL CRAYON, OR MELTED WAX CRAYON. WHEN THE MARACA IS FINISHED IT MAY BE USED AS A RHYTHM INSTRUMENT TO ACCENT WHATEVER BEAT OR TIMING THE YOUNGSTERS CHOOSE.

WHEN CONSIDERING THE MARACA, ONE SHOULD TAKE INTO ACCOUNT THAT IN THE LATIN AMERICAN MUSICAL EXPERIENCE, THERE ARE TWO WAYS IN WHICH THE MARACA IS USED ..... OFTEN YOU WILL SEE ONE MUSICIAN HANDLING TWO MARACAS, BUT THERE IS ALSO THE USE OF ONE MARACA (GENERALLY MUCH LARGER THAN ONE OF THOSE USED IN PAIRS) WHICH MIGHT ALSO BE CONSIDERED.

SUGGESTED GRADE LEVEL: INTERMEDIATE
                       ADVANCED

MATERIALS NEEDED (FOR EACH YOUNGSTER:)

1. ONE BALLOON (BASICALLY ROUND)
2. ONE CUP LIQUID STARCH
3. ONE CUP WATER
4. ONE CUP WHITE GLUE
5. ONE MIXING BOWL
6. ONE WIRE WHISK OR EGG BEATER
7. NEWSPAPER (TO BE TORN INTO STRIPS APPROXIMATELY 1" TO 2" WIDE)
8. TEMPERA PAINTS (ASSORTED COLORS)
9. OIL CRAYONS OR CRAY-PAS (ASSORTED COLORS)
10. WAX CRAYONS (WHICH MAY BE MELTED ::)
11. EASEL BRUSHES
12. TONGUE DEPRESSORS
13. ASSORTED DRIED VEGETABLES AND GRAINS (POPCORN ((POPPED AND UNPOPPED),) LIMA BEANS, PINTO BEANS, PEAS, BARLEY, BIRDSEED, ETC.)
14. PEBBLES
15. A SHORT LENGTH OF STRING OR RUBBER (ELASTIC) BANDS TO SECURE BALLOON FROM DEFLATING
16. A LENGTH OF WOODEN DOWEL (APPROXIMATELY $\frac{1}{2}$" IN DIAMETER AND ABOUT 8" LONG)

ACTIVITIES:

1. PLACE WHATEVER COMBINATION OF ITEMS YOU CHOOSE TO MAKE THE SOUND OF YOUR MARACA INTO THE BALLOON (DO THIS IN A SLOW AND CAREFUL MANNER ..... YOU WILL BE SURPRISED AT HOW MUCH THE BALLOON WILL ACCOMMODATE PROVIDED YOU DON'T FORCE THINGS)
2. BLOW UP THE BALLOON TO THE DESIRED SIZE
3. KNOT THE NECH OF THE BALLOON AND TIE THE NECK OF THE BALLOON TIGHTLY WITH EITHER STRING OR RUBBER (ELASTIC) BANDS
4. MIX THE WATER AND WHITE GLUE TO MAKE A THIN SOLUTION
5. ADD THE LIQUID STARCH SLOWLY, BEATING THE SOLUTION WHILE POURING THE LIQUID STARCH, WITH A WIRE WHISK OR EGG BEATER (THIS BLENDS, SMOOTHS, AND AERATES THE SOLUTION)
6. DIP NEWSPAPER STRIPS INTO THE MIXTURE AND BEGIN WRAPPING AROUND THE BALLOON INCLUDING THE NECK TO FORM AN EXTENSION

7. AFTER THE FIRST LAYER HAS BEEN COM-
PLETED, ATTACH THE WOODEN DOWEL TO
THE FORM BY INSERTING IT INTO THE NECK
OF THE BALLOON AND WRAP NEWSPAPER
STRIPS ABOUT THE UPPER PART OF THE
DOWEL ATTACHING IT TO THE BALLOON IT-
SELF (YOU MAY HAVE TO PROP THE DOWEL
UP WHILE THE INITIAL LAYERS DRY)

8. AFTER APPLYING TWO LAYERS OF THE PAPER
STRIPPING ALLOW TO DRY OVERNIGHT

9. REPEAT THE PROCESS APPLYING FOUR MORE
LAYERS FINISHING WITH A LAYER OF DRY
NEWSPAPER STRIPS WHICH WILL ADHERE
FROM THE EXCESS SOLUTION STILL ON THE
FORM

10. ALLOW TO DRY FOR AT LEAST TWENTY-FOUR
HOURS

11. WHEN THOROUGHLY DRY, CHECK THE
SECURITY OF THE HANDLE AND IF NEED BE
REINFORCE WITH MASKING TAPE, COVERING
THE TAPE WITH ONE MORE LAYER OF NEWS-
PAPER STRIPS

12. WHEN THOROUGHLY DRY THE COVERED
BALLOON WITH DRIED VEGETABLE, GRAINS,
OR PEBBLES INSIDE WILL RATTLE JUST
LIKE THE MATERIALS IN THE ORIGINAL
GOURDS USED IN MANY LATIN COUNTRIES AS
RHYTHM INSTRUMENTS

13. WHEN THE ENTIRE FORM IS THOROUGHLY DRY
IT MAY BE PAINTED AND/OR DECORATED
WITH ANY DESIGN OR COLOR THAT THE
YOUNGSTERS WISH TO EMPLOY

HINTS:

SHOULD THE YOUNGSTERS DECIDE TO USE OIL
CRAYONS OR CRAY-PAS, BE SURE THAT THEY
UNDERSTAND THAT THE BRIGHTEST AND MOST
VIBRANT COLORS ARE OBTAINED ONLY THROUGH
PRESSURE ON THE CRAYON SO THAT THE APPLI-
CATION OF COLOR IS AS THICK AS POSSIBLE.
IT IS ALSO POSSIBLE, ONCE THE BASE COLOR
IS APPLIED TO PAINT LIGHTLY OVER THE
SURFACE WITH A SOLUTION OF TURPENTINE
WHICH BREAKS DOWN THE COLOR AND ALLOWS IT
TO FLOW MORE SMOOTHLY

SHOULD YOUR YOUNGSTERS BE INTRIGUED WITH
THE POSSIBILITIES OF MELTED WAX CRAYON,
YOU MAY MAKE A DOUBLE-BOILER COOKER BY
USING A LARGE COFFEE CAN PARTIALLY FILLED
WITH WATER INTO WHICH SMALLER CANS CON-
TAINING THE DIFFERENT CRAYONS ARE PLACED.
HEAT UNTIL THE CRAYONS ARE MELTED SUFFIC-
IENTLY TO BE APPLIED TO THE FORM WITH A
TONGUE DEPRESSOR OR AN OLD BRUSH

14. WHEN COMPLETED, NOTE THAT THE CHOICES
OF FILL MATERIALS CREATE DIFFERENT
KINDS OF SOUNDS AND THAT THE MEDIA
CHOSEN TO DECORATE THE SURFACE ALSO
HAS AN EFFECT ON THIS SOUND

15. NOW YOU HAVE ENOUGH MARACAS TO FORM A
REAL RHYTHM BAND AND YOU CAN TRY
DIFFERENT RHYTHMS WITH DIFFERENT
FAMILIAR MELODIES

NOTES FOR THE TEACHER

MARACAS ARE A NATURAL RHYTHM INSTRUMENT USED BY MANY PRIMITIVE PEOPLE. ORIGINALLY THEY WERE GOURDS WHICH HAD BEEN ALLOWED TO DRY SUFFICIENTLY TO LOOSEN THE SEEDS INSIDE. NOW, THEY ARE OFTEN MADE FROM LAQUERED WOOD OR, MORE COMMONLY (ESPECIALLY FOR THE TOURIST TRADE) PLASTIC NEITHER OF WHICH REALLY PRODUCE THE SOUND THEY SHOULD.

THE USE OF MARACAS IS MORE HIGHLY IDENTIFIED WITH LATIN RHYTHMS THAN WITH ANY OTHER MUSIC.

CHILDREN MAY BENEFIT FROM MAKING AND USING SUCH INSTRUMENTS AS AIDS TO PSYCHO-MOTOR DEVELOPMENT, COUNTING AND ACCENTING RHYTHMS, AND THE PLEASURE OF HAVING MADE, ACTUALLY CREATED, THEIR OWN MUSICAL INSTRUMENT.

PEANUT (GROUNDNUT, EARTHNUT, GOOBER), DE-
SPITE ITS SEVERAL COMMON NAMES, IS NOT A
TRUE NOT BUT THE POD OR LEGUME OF ARACHIS
HUPOGAEA, WHICH HAS THE PECULIAR HABIT OF
RIPENING UNDERGROUND. IT IS A CONCENTRATED
FOOD: POUND FOR POUND PEANUTS HAVE MORE
PROTEIN, MINERALS, AND VITAMINS THAN BEEF
LIVER; MORE FAT THAN HEAVY CREAM; MORE FOOD
ENERGY (CALORIES) THAN SUGAR. NATIVE TO
SOUTH AMERICA, THE PEANUT WAS, EARLY ON,
INTRODUCED INTO THE OLD WORLD TROPICS.
INDIA, CHINA, WEST AFRICA, AND THE UNITED
STATES HAVE BECOME THE LARGEST COMMERCIAL
PRODUCERS OF PEANUTS.   THERE ARE THREE
MAJOR PEANUT PRODUCING REGIONS IN THE
UNITED STATES: VIRGINIA-CAROLINA GROWS
MAINLY THE LARGE VIRGINIA TYPE; GEORGIA-
FLORIDA-ALABAMA GROWS THE SOUTHEASTERN
RUNNER, VIRGINIA, AND SPANISH TYPES; AND
OKLAHOMA-TEXAS GROWS MAINLY THE SPANISH
TYPE.
PROFITABLE GROWING OF PEANUTS REQUIRES AT
LEAST FIVE MONTHS OF WARM WEATHER WITH A
STEADY SUPPLY OF MOISTURE. IN ASIA THE
PEANUTS ARE GROWN UNDER CONSTANT IRRIGATION.
PEANUTS ARE GROWN MAINLY FOR THE EDIBLE OIL
EXCEPT FOR IN THE UNITED STATES WHERE HALF
THE HARVESTED CROP PRODUCTION IS GROUND AND
MADE INTO PEANUT BUTTER AND THE REST FOR
ROASTED, SALTED NUTS; AND FOR USE IN CANDY
AND BAKERY PRODUCTS WITH 10% TO 12% OF THE
CROP USED FOR PEANUT OIL.   IN THE SOUTHERN
UNITED STATES THE PEANUT IS USED TO A SMALL
DEGREE TO FEED LIVESTOCK.   THE TOPS OF THE
PLANTS ARE LARGELY RETURNED TO THE SOIL
INCIDENTAL TO REMOVAL OF THE PODS BY A
MOBIL HARVESTER.

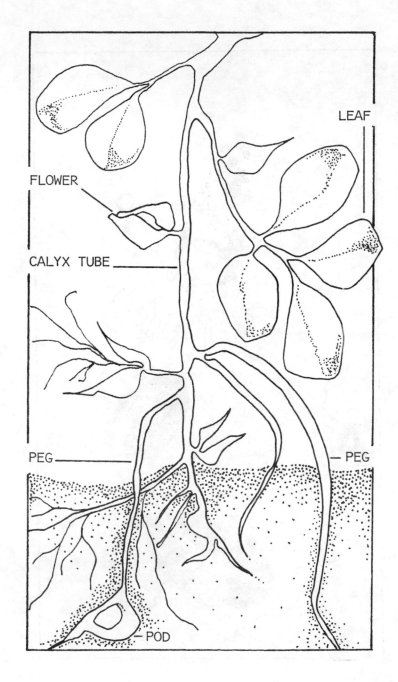

A MINIATURE PEANUT FARM

THIS ACTIVITY TAKES APPROXIMATELY FOUR MONTHS TO BRING TO FRUITION AND CORRELATES DIRECTLY WITH THE FOLLOWING SUGGESTED ACTIVITY.

IT IS OUR SUGGESTION THAT THIS ACTIVITY BE REGARDED AS A CONTINUING SCIENCE PROJECT AND THAT THE FACILITIES OF OBSERVATION AND REPORTING (RECORDING) BE ENCOURAGED AND DEVELOPED.

SUGGESTED GRADE LEVEL: PRIMARY
                               INTERMEDIATE
                               ADVANCED

MATERIALS NEEDED:

1. A BAG OF RAW (SHELLED) PEANUTS (THE AMOUNT DEPENDS UPON THE AVAILABLE PLANTING AREA, GROWING SEASON LENGTH, LIGHT SOURCE, ETC ..... BUT AT LEAST ONE PER STUDENT)
2. A GARDEN PLOT WITH ENOUGH ROOM TO PLANT THE PEANUTS APPROXIMATELY TWO OR THREE INCHES APART IN ROWS ARRANGED THIRTY TO THIRTY-SIX INCHES APART

OR .....

1. AN EMPTY MILK CARTON FOR EACH YOUNGSTER TO USE AS A PLANTER (A QUART SIZED CARTON IS BEST)
2. SANDY SOIL
3. SMALL ROCKS
4. WATER

ACTIVITIES:

1. CUT OFF THE TOP (ABOUT HALF) OF THE QUART SIZED MILK CARTON
2. PUT SOME ROCKS IN THE BOTTOM
2. PUT SOME ROCKS IN THE BOTTOM FOR DRAINAGE
3. FILL THE CONTAINER APPROXIMATELY HALF FULL WITH SOIL
4. DROP A RAW (SHELLED) PEANUT INTO THE CONTAINER
5. WATER WELL
6. PLACE IN A WARM, SUNNY SPOT
7. WATER A LITTLE BIT EACH DAY
8. AS THE PLANT BEGINS TO GROW, YOU WILL PROBABLY NEED A SMALL STAKE IN EACH CARTON (OR PLANTING BED) TO SUPPORT THE VINE WHICH WILL GROW TO ABOUT TWELVE TO SIXTEEN INCHES
9. WATCH FOR THE SMALL GOLDEN-YELLOW FLOWERS WHICH WILL DEVELOP ALONG THE VINE
10. AFTER THE FLOWERS WITHER AND DIE, HEAVY STALKS WILL BEGIN TO APPEAR AND THESE STALKS WILL GROW DOWN INTO THE SOIL
11. THE TIP OF EACH STALK DEVELOPS INTO A SMALL POD AND LATER INTO A FULL-SIZED PEANUT
12. AFTER THE PLANT BEGINS TO DRY AND WITHER, THE PEANUTS ARE READY TO HARVEST
13. THE SAME GENERAL ROUTINE IS FOLLOWED IN THE CASE OF OUT OF DOORS PLANTING

NOTES FOR THE TEACHER

THIS IS A MARVELOUS ACTIVITY TO DEEPLY INVOLVE EACH YOUNGSTER IN THE GROWTH AND DEVELOPMENT OF HIS OR HER OWN PLANT. IT IS AN IDEAL WAY OF STRESSING THE SCIENTIFIC METHODS OF OBSERVATION AND REPORTING IN WHICH EACH OF THE YOUNGSTERS CAN KEEP A PERSONAL RECORD OF THE DEVELOPMENT OF EACH PLANT.

IT NEED NOT BE RESTRICTED TO PEANUTS ..... THE TOPS OF CARROTS PLACED IN WATER, PART OF A SWEET POTATO PLACED IN SUGARED WATER, THE SEED (PIT) OF AN AVOCADO PIERCED WITH TOOTHPICKS AND SET IN WATER, ETC. ALL ALLOW FOR THIS VITAL KIND OF EXPERIENCE.

MAKING PEANUT AND YAM STEW

THIS ACTIVITY, WHICH CAN EASILY BE PRE-
PARED IN AN HOUR, COMBINES THE SCIENCE
CONCEPTS FROM THE PRECEEDING ACTIVITY WITH
FACTS ABOUT NUTRITION, BLACK HISTORY, AND
CURRENT POLITICAL SCIENCE. IN ADDITION,
FOR MANY OF THE YOUNGSTERS, THIS WILL BE
THE CLOSEST THEY CAN COME TO THE FEELING
A FARMER MUST HAVE OF SEEING THAT WHICH HE
HAS PLANTED TURNED INTO THAT WHICH SUS-
TAINS HIM.

SUGGESTED GRADE LEVEL: PRIMARY
                        INTERMEDIATE
                        ADVANCED

MATERIALS NEEDED:

1. YAMS ..... ENOUGH FOR EACH MEMBER OF
    THE CLASS TO HAVE AT LEAST ONE GOOD
    HELPING (FIVE POUNDS OF YAMS WILL
    GENERALLY SERVE BETWEEN TWELVE AND
    FOURTEEN PEOPLE)
2. A LARGE COOKING POT
3. SALT
4. RAW (SHELLED) PEANUTS (APPROXIMATELY
    ¼ CUP OF SHELLED PEANUTS PER POUND OF
    YAMS)

ACTIVITIES:

1. WITH THE YOUNGEST CHILDREN GO ON A
    FIELD TRIP TO THE GROCERY OR PRODUCE
    MARKET TO BUY YAMS ..... WITH THE
    MORE ADVANCED YOUNGSTERS HAVE EACH
    OBTAIN TWO YAMS AND BRING THEM TO
    CLASS (BE VERY SURE THAT THE YOUNGSTER
    IS AWARE OF THE DIFFERENCE BETWEEN A
    YAM AND A SWEET POTATO)

2. SCRUB THE YAMS BUT DO NOT PEEL THEM
3. COOK THE YAMS IN BOILING WATER (WITH
    SALT ADDED) FOR APPROXIMATELY TWENTY
    MINUTES
4. DRAIN OFF APPROXIMATELY 2/3 OF THE
    LIQUID AND SAVE THE REST FOR FURTHER
    COOKING
5. PEEL THE COOKED YAMS AND CUT THEM INTO
    SMALL PIECES OR MASH THEM WITH A
    POTATO MASHER
6. MIX THE RAW PEANUTS IN WITH THE YAMS
7. RETURN THE MIXTURE TO THE COOKING POT,
    ADD SALT TO SUIT YOUR TASTE AND COOK
    FOR ANOTHER FIVE TO TEN MINUTES .....

    OR .....

8. IF YOU HAVE ACCESS TO AN OVEN, YOU CAN
    BAKE THE MIXTURE FOR FIVE TO TEN
    MINUTES AT FOUR HUNDRED DEGREES WHICH
    WILL PRODUCE A DELICATE BROWN TOP
9. SERVE PORTIONS IN SMALL BOWLS

NOTES FOR THE TEACHER

SINCE THE PEANUT IS RICH IN OIL AND VITAMINS, IT IS A VERY IMPORTANT PART OF THE DIET IN MANY COUNTRIES ..... TROPICAL SOUTH AMERICA, INDIA, CHINA, WEST AFRICA, AND THE SOUTHERN PART OF THE UNITED STATES ALL OF WHICH RELY HEAVILY ON THE PEANUT AND ITS OIL.

ALMOST EIGHTY YEARS AGO, A BLACK BOTANIST, GEORGE WASHINGTON CARVER, PERSUADED FARMERS IN ALABAMA, GEORGIA, AND OTHER SOUTHERN STATES TO RAISE SOMETHING OTHER THAN COTTON. REPEATED PLANTING AND HARVESTING OF COTTON WAS WEARING OUT THE SOIL AND, TO ALLOW THE SOIL TO RECUPERATE FROM SUCH USE, CARVER SHOWED THE FARMERS HOW TO RAISE PEANUTS AND ALSO YAMS.

FROM THE PEANUT HE DEVELOPED CHEESE, MILK, COFFEE, FLOUR, SOAP, AND EVEN DYE AND INSULATING BOARD MADE FROM PEANUT FIBRE.

FROM THE YAM HE DEVELOPED SUGAR, VINEGAR, MOLASSES, AND EVEN RUBBER.

AS ANYONE CAN READILY SEE, GEORGE WASHINGTON CARVER DID MUCH TOWARD CHANGING THE FARMING HABITS OF THE SOUTH, INCREASING THE YIELD, AND REPLENISHING THE SOIL. HIS LIFE WOULD BE AN ADMIRABLE STUDY FOR ANY YOUNGSTER.

FROM HIS AFRICAN HERITAGE GEORGE WASHINGTON CARVER LEARNED THAT PEANUTS AND YAMS ARE NOT ONLY EXCELLENT CROPS TO ENRICH WORN OUT SOIL, BUT ALSO, WHEN THEY ARE COOKED TOGETHER, THEY ARE ABSOLUTELY DELICIOUS AND, FURTHER, THE COMBINATION OF

THE TWO PROVIDE THE BODY WITH MINERALS AND OILS ESSENTIAL TO GROWTH AND DEVELOPMENT.

FOR COUNTRIES WHICH DO NOT HAVE SUFFICIENT MEAT TO FEED THEIR POPULATIONS, THE PEANUT AND YAM ARE VITAL AS DAILY FOOD PROVIDING A NOURISHING STAPLE WHICH, IN LARGE MEASURE CAN AND DOES, REPLACE WHAT THEY LACK.

HUSH PUPPIES

BREADS AND BATTER MADE FROM CORN MEAL WERE AMONG THE FIRST BASIC FOODS IN THE OLD SOUTH.

WHEN THE BLACK COOKS ON THE PLANTATIONS WERE BUSY PREPARING MEALS, THE HUNTING DOGS WOULD GATHER ROUND THE AREA WHERE THE SMELL WAS SO ENTICING AND WHINE FOR FOOD. TO KEEP THEM QUIET, THE COOKS WOULD MAKE SMALL BALLS OF CORNMEAL DOUGH, FRY THEM QUICKLY, AND TOSS THEM TO THE DOGS, CALLING OUT, "HUSH, YOU PUPPY!" THE DOGS WOULD QUIET AFTER THEY HAD BEEN SATISFIED.

SUGGESTED GRADE LEVEL: PRIMARY
                        INTERMEDIATE
                        ADVANCED

MATERIALS NEEDED: (TO MAKE ABOUT THIRTY)

1. TEASPOON/TABLESPOON MEASURE
2. CUP MEASURE
3. DEEP FRY PAN
4. MIXING SPOON
5. HOT PLATE-ELECTRIC OR ACCESS TO SCHOOL STOVE OR HOME ECONOMICS DEPARTMENT STOVE OR ELECTRIC FRY PAN
6. 1½ CUPS CORN MEAL
7. 1½ CUPS WATER
8. 1/3 CUP MILK
9. 1 TABLESPOON VEGETABLE OIL
10. 2 TEASPOONS GRATED ONION
11. 2 EGGS - BEATEN
12. 1 CUP FLOUR
13. 3 TEASPOONS BAKING POWDER
14. 2 TEASPOONS SALT

ACTIVITIES:

1. COMBINE CORN MEAL AND WATER AND COOK STIRRING UNTIL STIFF
2. REMOVE FROM HEAT
3. ADD MILK, OIL, AND ONION AND STIR UNTIL THE MIXTURE IS SMOOTH
4. GRADUALLY ADD BEATEN EGGS INTO THE MIXTURE
5. ADD FLOUR AND BLEND THOROUGHLY
6. HEAT ENOUGH COOKING OIL TO COVER SMALL BALLS OF MIXTURE UNTIL THE OIL IS UP TO FRYING TEMPERATURE
7. ROLL SMALL BALLS OF CORNMEAL DOUGH AND DROP THEM INTO THE HOT OIL
8. ALLOW THEM TO COOK FOR APPROXIMATELY FIVE OR SIX MINUTES
9. DRAIN THE "HUSH PUPPIES" ON PAPER TOWELS BEFORE ALLOWING THE YOUNGSTERS TO EAT THEM.

NOTES FOR THE TEACHER

THIS ACTIVITY INVOLVES HISTORY, GEOGRAPHY, MATH, AND – ABOVE ALL – FOOD! THE TITLE ALONE SHOULD INTRIGUE MOST YOUNGSTERS WHO WILL PROBABLY HAVE HAD AN ENTIRELY DIFFERENT EXPERIENCE WITH THE TERM HUSH PUPPIES.

AS A FOLLOW-UP ACTIVITY YOU MIGHT EXPLAIN HOW EARLY KITCHENS IN THE SOUTHERN COLONIES WERE HOUSED IN A SEPARATE UNIT WHICH WAS CONNECTED TO THE MAIN HOUSE AND DINING ROOM BY A SHORT, COVERED WALKWAY. IN THE NORTHERN COLONIES, THE KITCHENS WERE USUALLY IN THE BASEMENT AND FOOD WAS TRANSPORTED FROM KITCHEN TO DINING ROOM BY A SMALL, HAND-OPERATED, ELEVATOR.

THE BASIC IDEA WAS, IN BOTH INSTANCES, TO KEEP KITCHEN ODORS OUT OF THE MAIN PART OF THE HOUSE. THERE WERE NO EXHAUST FANS OR AIR CONDITIONING UNITS THEN AND THE ODOR OF FRIED FISH AND THE LIKE COULD LINGER FOR DAYS.

CALZONES / MEXICAN "PANTS" BISCUITS

FOOD IS UNIVERSAL LANGUAGE, USED IDIOMAT-
ICALLY IN EACH CULTURE, BUT ALWAYS TOWARD
THE SAME END: TO SATISFY HUNGER AND PROVIDE
A SENSE OF WELL-BEING AND CARING. THERE IS
NO WAY YOU CAN HOPE TO DUPLICATE THE
FEELING THAT IS GENERATED BY A MEXICAN
FAMILY AS THEY SHARE A MEAL BUT "BREAKING
BREAD" TOGETHER CAN GO A LONG WAY IN
GENERATING A GOOD FEELING TOWARD AND AMONG
DIFFERENT ETHNIC CULTURES.

SUGGESTED GRADE LEVEL: PRIMARY
                             INTERMEDIATE
                             ADVANCED

MATERIALS NEEDED: (TO MAKE ABOUT FIFTY)

1. TEASPOON/TABLESPOON MEASURE
2. CUP MEASURE
3. SIFTER
4. LARGE MIXING BOWL
5. ROLLING PIN
6. LARGE BREADBOARD
7. SHARP KNIFE
8. 4 OR 5 COOKIE/BAKING SHEETS
9. PORTABLE OVEN OR ACCESS TO SCHOOL
   OVENS OR HOME ECONOMICS DEPARTMENT
   OVENS
10. ½ CUP PLUS 2 TABLESPOONS SHORTENING
11. 7 TABLESPOONS SUGAR
12. 4 CUPS REGULAR ALL-PURPOSE FLOUR
13. 5 TEASPOONS BAKING POWDER
14. 1 TEASPOON SALT
15. 1¼ CUPS MILK
16. ¼ CUP SUGAR
17. ¼ TEASPOON CINNAMON

ACTIVITIES:

1. CREAM THE SHORTENING AND SUGAR UNTIL FLUFFY
2. SIFT THE FLOUR, MEASURE, THEN SIFT AGAIN ADDING BAKING POWDER AND SALT AND SIFT ONCE MORE
3. GRADUALLY ADD THE DRY INGREDIENTS TO THE CREAMED MIXTURE ALTERNATING WITH SMALL INCREMENTS OF MILK, MIXING THE INGREDIENTS UNTIL WELL BLENDED
4. KNEAD THE RESULTING DOUGH AND ROLL OUT ON A LIGHTLY FLOURED BREAD BOARD TO A SHEET ABOUT ¼" THICK
5. FOR THE BISCUITS ..... WITH A SHARP-POINTED KNIFE, CUT OUT A RECTANGLE OF DOUGH AND MODIFY SO THAT YOU HAVE A BASE ABOUT 1½ INCHES WIDE, SIDES ABOUT 2¼ INCHES HIGH AND THE TOP ABOUT 1¼ INCHES WIDE.
6. CUT A SMALL V SHAPE FROM THE TOP AND USE YOUR IMAGINATION AS TO HOW THE "LEGS" SHOULD BE HANDLED (THERE ARE POSSIBILITIES DIAGRAMMED BELOW)
7. PUT THE BISCUITS ON A GREASED COOKIE SHEET AND BAKE FOR APPROXIMATELY FIFTEEN TO TWENTY MINUTES AT 350 DEGREES.
8. SOME "BAKERS" PREFER TO SPRINKLE SUGAR AND CINNAMON ONTO THE PASTRIES BEFORE BAKING, OTHERS WAIT UNTIL AFTER. TRY IT BOTH WAYS!

NOTES FOR THE TEACHER

THIS ACTIVITY WILL APPEAL TO YOUNGSTERS
FOR TWO REASONS: FIRST BECAUSE OF THE
UNUSUAL SHAPE OF THE PASTRY AND SECONDLY,
BECAUSE THEY ARE VERY MUCH LIKE AMERICAN
SUGAR COOKIES.

THE WORD CALZONES (KAHL-SOH-NEHS) WILL GIVE
THEM A NEW SPANISH WORD FOR THEIR MULTI-
CULTURAL VOCABULARY. IT MEANS, LITERALLY,
"LITTLE BRITCHES!"

THE ACTIVITY ALSO INTEGRATES MATH
(MEASURING, TEMPERATURE,) AND SAFETY
(USE OF HEAT AND COOKING UTENSILS.)

HAIKU POETRY

THIS ACTIVITY IS DESIGNED TO DEMONSTRATE
THE JAPANESE USE OF SHORT, SIMPLE, RHYME-
LESS POEMS TO EMPHASIZE THE BEAUTY OF
NATURE AND THE POWERFUL CONTENT OF SIMPLE
AND UNCOMPLICATED WORDS.

SUGGESTED GRADE LEVEL: PRIMARY
                              INTERMEDIATE
                              ADVANCED

MATERIALS NEEDED:

1. PAPER
2. PENCIL OR PEN
3. RICE PAPER
4. A SMALL PAINT BRUSH
5. BLACK INK (INDIA INK OR JAPANESE INK)
6. A WATER CONTAINER
7. PAPER TOWELS

ACTIVITIES:

1. DEMONSTRATE, WITH EXAMPLES, THE BASIC
   ANATOMY OF THE HAIKU ..... A THREE
   LINE POEM, CONTAINING A TOTAL OF
   SEVENTEEN SYLLABLES ARRANGED IN LINES
   OF FIVE, SEVEN, AND FIVE SYLLABLES
   RESPECTIVELY

2. USING THE CHENOWETH :: EXAMPLE .....

         AN OLD PATCHWORK QUILT
   BROOMS AND SMALL HANDS MAKE A TENT –
         AN ARCHITECT DREAMS!

   ..... ENCOURAGE THE YOUNGSTERS TO
   BECOME AWARE OF THE UNDERSTATEMENT
   ACHIEVED BY THE CAREFUL USE OF WORDS
   AND POINT OUT THAT EACH WORD IS
   IMPORTANT AND MUST BE CHOSEN WITH CARE.

3. NOTE THAT IN MOST HAIKU THE FIRST TWO
   LINES (TWELVE SYLLABLES) ARE USUALLY A
   STATEMENT OF A SITUATION OR THE DE-
   SCRIPTION OF A SCENE, WHILE THE LAST
   LINE (FIVE SYLLABLES) DRAWS A CON-
   CLUSION OR DESCRIBES AN ACTION; BUT
   MOST ESPECIALLY, IT DRAWS A SOMEWHAT
   UNEXPECTED CONTRAST

4. THE WORKING OUT OF EACH OF THE INDIVID-
   UAL HAIKUS SHOULD BE DONE ON NEWSPRINT
   OR STANDARD WRITING TABLET, BUT ONCE
   THE FORM IS SOLIDIFIED, IF THE YOUNG-
   STERS WISH TO PRESENT THE HAIKU IN THE
   TRADITIONAL JAPANESE STYLE EACH SHOULD
   HAVE A PIECE OF RICE PAPER ON WHICH
   HE WRITES OR LETTERS HIS HAIKU AND TO
   WHICH HE ADDS SOME DECORATIVE TREAT-
   MENT IN THE MANNER OF THE "SUMI PAINT-
   ERS"

5. THE ESSENCE OF "SUMI" IS, LIKE THE
   HAIKU, SIMPLICITY, THAT REMARKABLE
   ABILITY TO SUGGEST MUCH WITH VERY
   LITTLE ..... THE OLD MASTERS ARE ABLE
   TO DO THIS WITH A VARIETY OF INTRICATE
   SHADINGS IN THEIR BLACK AND WHITE WORK
   BUT FOR MOST YOUNGSTERS IT IS ENOUGH
   IF THEY ARE ABLE TO KEEP THEIR COM-
   POSITIONS SIMPLE, UNCLUTTERED, AND TO
   A MINIMUM OF LINES

6. THE BRUSH MUST DO ALL OF THE WORK AND
   THE "TRICK" IS TO REMEMBER THAT THERE
   CAN BE NO OUTLINE ..... YOU DRAW
   NOTHING ..... THE COMPOSITION HAPPENS
   BY THE AMOUNT OF PRESSURE THE YOUNG-
   STER APPLIES TO THE BRUSH AND THE
   DIRECTION HIS LINES TAKE

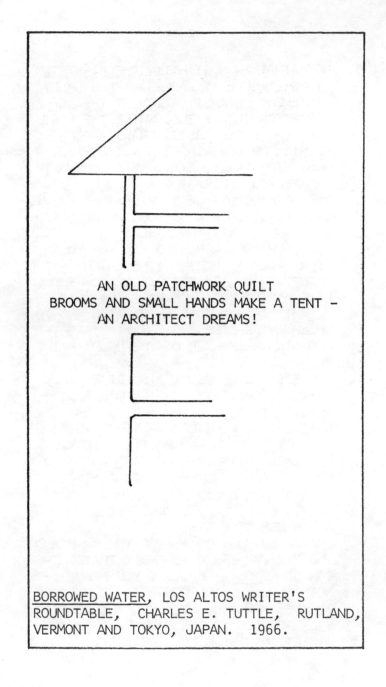

AN OLD PATCHWORK QUILT
BROOMS AND SMALL HANDS MAKE A TENT —
AN ARCHITECT DREAMS!

BORROWED WATER, LOS ALTOS WRITER'S
ROUNDTABLE, CHARLES E. TUTTLE, RUTLAND,
VERMONT AND TOKYO, JAPAN. 1966.

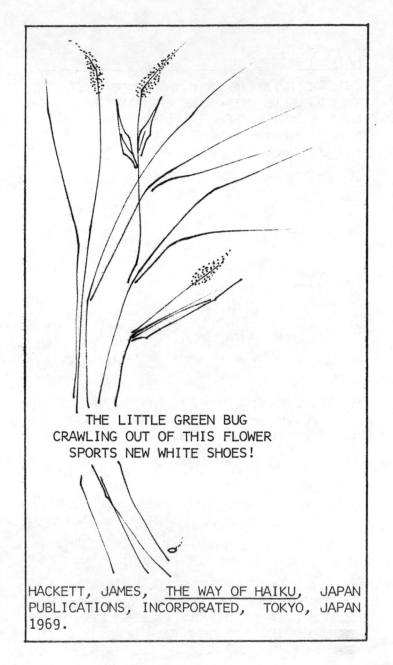

THE LITTLE GREEN BUG
CRAWLING OUT OF THIS FLOWER
SPORTS NEW WHITE SHOES!

HACKETT, JAMES, THE WAY OF HAIKU, JAPAN
PUBLICATIONS, INCORPORATED, TOKYO, JAPAN
1969.

NOTES FOR THE TEACHER

HAIKU IS A UNIQUE FORM OF POETIC EXPRES-
SION WHICH ONE JAPANESE WRITER DESCRIBES
AS " ..... A WILLOW BRANCH ..... TREMBLING
A LITTLE IN THE WIND. "

ONCE YOUNG PEOPLE GET THE FEEL OF SEVEN-
TEEN SYLLABLES AND THE ABSENCE OF RHYMING,
THEY WILL EXPRESS SOME SURPRISINGLY
BEAUTIFUL THOUGHTS.

THERE ARE SEVERAL "HINTS" WHICH YOU MIGHT
FIND OF HELP IN WORKING THROUGH THIS
ACTIVITY WHICH WE WOULD LIKE TO SHARE WITH
YOU .....

A FEW DAYS BEFORE YOU PLAN TO START THIS
ACTIVITY, SET TWO FLOWER ARRANGEMENTS IN
PROMINANT PLACES IN THE CLASSROOM. ONE
SUCH ARRANGEMENT SHOULD BE A TRADITIONAL
WESTERN BOUQUET, THE OTHER A SIMPLE CON-
TAINER WITH ONE BEAUTIFUL FLOWER AND
PERHAPS ONE SPRIG OF GRASS OR BIT OF FERN
IN THE JAPANESE STYLE. DO NOT CALL
ATTENTION TO EITHER ..... ALLOW THE YOUNG-
STERS TO "LIVE WITH THEM."

WHEN BEGINNING THE HAIKU ACTIVITY YOU
MIGHT CALL ATTENTION TO THE CONTRAST
BETWEEN THE TWO, INDICATING THE SIMPLICITY
OF THE JAPANESE STYLE AS OPPOSED TO THE
MORE COMPLEX COMPOSITION OF THE WESTERN
BOUQUET. DRAW THE COMPARISON BETWEEN
THE SPARE AND CAREFUL USE OF WORDS IN
HAIKU, AND THE SPARE AND CAREFUL USE OF
FLOWERS, ETC. IN THE IKEBANA (JAPANESE)
FLOWER ARRANGEMENT.

THIS COMPARATIVE MIGHT BE DRAWN TO ALL
AREAS OF JAPANESE AND WESTERN LIFE .....
CLOTHING, FURNITURE, FOOD PREPARATION AND
PRESENTATION, ETC.

ENCOURAGE THE YOUNGSTERS TO OBSERVE NATURE
ALL ABOUT THEM AND RECOGNIZE THE MANY
THINGS WE LOOK AT EVERY DAY BUT NEVER
REALLY SEE.

WHEN ACTUALLY INVOLVED IN THE MECHANICS OF
HAIKU COMPOSITION HERE ARE A FEW HINTS
WHICH MIGHT COME IN HANDY IF YOU STRESS
THEM TO YOUR YOUNGSTERS OCASSIONALLY .....

USE ALL VERBS IN THE PRESENT TENSE .....
THE PRESENT IS WHAT HAIKU IS ALL ABOUT!

CHOOSE WORDS CAREFULLY ..... BE SURE THAT
THEY EXPRESS PRECISELY WHAT YOU FEEL AND
DON'T WORRY ABOUT USING A WORD IN A WAY
THAT IT HAS NEVER BEEN USED BEFORE .....
THAT IS WHAT CREATIVITY IS ALL ABOUT AND
YOU HAVE ARTISTIC LICENSE!

AVOID RHYME ..... HAIKU IS ANTI-RHYME!

REVISE AND REWRITE YOUR THREE LINE FORM
UNTIL IT SOUNDS GOOD TO YOUR EAR AND
FEELS GOOD ON YOUR TONGUE!

TEACHER'S NOTES

INDIAN DANCE COLLAR

THIS ACTIVITY IS DESIGNED TO PROVIDE THE YOUNGSTERS WITH, AT LEAST, A SMALL VICARIOUS EXPERIENCE IN TRADITIONAL NATIVE AMERICAN DRESS.

THE CEREMONIAL COLLAR IS USED BY MANY TRIBES AND IS USUALLY MADE FROM BONES OR SHELLS AND IS DECORATED IN ANY NUMBER OF WAYS WITH BRIGHTLY COLORED BEADS, OR FEATHERS, OR STONES, OR A COMBINATION OF ALL THESE MATERIALS.

NATIVE AMERICANS CONSIDERED SUCH ARTICLES AN INTEGRAL PART OF THEIR LIFE. OFTEN EACH ARTICLE USED HAD SPECIFIC AND VERY DEFINITE MEANING ON A SYMBOLIC LEVEL.

TODAY SUCH ARTICLES ARE GENERALLY CLASS-IFIED AS JEWELRY AND HAVE FORMED THE BASIS FOR SOME EXCEPTIONALLY BEAUTIFUL AND EX-CEEDINGLY EXPENSIVE NECKLACES.

IN ADDITION TO THE DESIGN POSSIBILITIES WHICH ARE INHERENT IN THIS ACTIVITY, THERE IS ALSO A STRONG MATH CORRELATION PRESENT AS WELL AS EXERCISE IN MOTOR COORDINATION.

SUGGESTED GRADE LEVEL: INTERMEDIATE
ADVANCED

MATERIALS NEEDED:

1. PLAIN WHITE SODA STRAWS
2. COLORED YARN (AS LARGE AN ASSORTMENT AS POSSIBLE)
3. COLORED GLASS BEADS (A LARGE ASSORT-MENT)
4. COLORED WOODEN BEADS (A LARGE ASSORT-MENT)
5. SMALL STONES (WITH HOLES DRILLED)
6. RULERS
7. A TAPE MEASURE
8. SCISSORS
9. TAPESTRY NEEDLES (WITH LARGE EYES)

ACTIVITIES:

1. HAVE EACH YOUNGSTER MEASURE AROUND HIS NECK TO DETERMINE HOW LONG THE COLLAR SHOULD BE TO FIT COMFORTABLY
2. EACH YOUNGSTER SHOULD ALSO MEASURE THE WIDTH OF HIS NECK TO DETERMINE HOW MANY ROWS OF STRAWS HE CAN FIT UNDER HIS CHIN, COMFORTABLY
3. CUT THE SODA STRAWS INTO TWO INCH PIECES
4. AFTER THE YOUNGSTERS HAVE CHOSEN WHICH COLOR YARN EACH WILL USE, HAVE EACH THREAD THE YARN ONTO A TAPESTRY NEEDLE
5. THREAD, ALTERNATELY, A PIECE OF SODA STRAW AND A BEAD (OR BEADS) ON A LENGTH OF YARN
6. WHEN ONE LENGTH IS COMPLETED, TIE A KNOT AT THE END TO KEEP THAT ROW SECURE AND BEGIN ON THE NEXT ROW
7. WHEN THE YOUNGSTER HAS COMPLETED ROWS ENOUGH TO MAKE HIS COLLAR FIT COMFORT-ABLY, KNOT THE ENTIRE END ASSEMBLY AND LEAVE ENOUGH YARN TO TIE INTO A BOW IN THE BACK TO ACT AS A CATCH
8. EACH CHILD SHOULD HAVE SOMETHING LIKE THIS .....

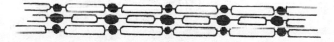

9. THERE ARE OTHER POSSIBILITIES WHICH
    MAY BE CONSIDERED ONCE THE BASIC
    COLLAR IS CONSTRUCTED .....
    A) FEATHERS MIGHT BE SECURED TO PARTS
       OF THE COLLAR TO ENHANCE THE
       DESIGN (WHITE GLUE IS MOST EFFECT-
       IVE WITH FEATHERS)
    B) SMALL BITS OF SHINY GLASS MAY BE
       SECURED TO PARTS OF THE COLLAR
       (AIRPLANE GLUE WORKS BEST FOR THIS
       BUT BE SURE THE ROOM IS WELL
       VENTILATED SHOULD YOU DECIDE TO USE
       IT
    C) PENDENTS MAY BE CONSTRUCTED IN THE
       SAME MANNER AS THE BASIC COLLAR AND
       TIED TO THE LOWEST ROW OF THE
       COLLAR TO HANG DOWN

NOTES FOR THE TEACHER

THERE ARE COUNTLESS VARIATIONS ON THE
CEREMONIAL COLLAR. SOME WERE ELABORATELY
CARVED FROM STONE AND, LATER, PRECIOUS
METALS AND WERE DECORATED WITH MANY
DIFFERENT KINDS OF "BANGLES" AND "BEADS,"
FEATHERS, ARROW HEADS, ANIMAL TEETH, SHORT
LENGTHS OF LEATHER, AND PRECIOUS STONES.
THE ONLY THING WHICH HELD THE FLAMBOYANCE,
THEATRICALITY, AND/OR ELEGANCE BACK WAS
THE INDIVIDUAL CREATIVITY OF THE CREATOR.

IN ITS SIMPLEST FORM THIS ACTIVITY COULD
BE USED WITH PRIMARY LEVEL YOUNGSTERS BUT
IS FAR MORE EFFECTIVE WITH OLDER CHILDREN,
AND WITH ADVANCED YOUNGSTERS YOU MIGHT
ENCOURAGE RESEARCH TO DETERMINE AUTHENTIC
DESIGNS AND MATERIALS USED BY VARIOUS
INDIAN TRIBES.

WITH THE CONTEMPORARY INTEREST AND ENTHUS-
IASM FOR INDIAN DESIGN AND EMPHASIS IN
JEWELRY, THERE IS A GREAT DEAL OF INFOR-
MATION AVAILABLE AND AN ENTHUSIASTIC
AUDIENCE FOR IT.

THE AMERICAN MOSAIC

THIS ACTIVITY IS DESIGNED TO INVOLVE EACH
OF THE YOUNGSTERS IN A GROUP PROJECT WHICH
WILL EVOLVE AS A DIRECT RESULT OF INDIVID-
UAL EFFORTS. EACH YOUNGSTER CREATES HIS
OWN CONTRIBUTION TO A GROUP COMPOSITION,
DOING HIS OWN RESEARCH AND CREATIVE WORK
TOWARD THAT END.

AS A RESULT OF THIS ACTIVITY EACH OF THE
YOUNGSTER'S RESEARCH SKILLS WILL BE DE-
VELOPED AS WILL HIS MOTOR SKILLS AND
CREATIVE IMAGINATION. THE ESSENCE OF THE
ACTIVITY IS TO ENCOURAGE THE YOUNGSTER'S
FACILITY WITH AND SKILL AT TRANSFORMING
INFORMATION WHICH IS ESSENTIALLY INTELLECT-
UAL INTO VISUAL TERMS.

SUGGESTED GRADE LEVEL: PRIMARY
                       INTERMEDIATE
                       ADVANCED

MATERIALS NEEDED:

1. TWO SHEETS OF BUTCHER PAPER APPROX-
   IMATELY 3'X5' FOR EVERY TEN YOUNGSTERS
   INVOLVED IN THE PROJECT
2. FELT TIP MARKING PENS (ASSORTED POINT
   WIDTHS, SIZES, AND COLORS)
3. SCISSORS
4. MAGAZINES
5. PHOTOGRAPHS (PERSONAL SNAPSHOTS IF THE
   STUDENT WOULD LIKE TO USE THEM)
6. COLORED CONSTRUCTION PAPER (12X18"
   ASSORTED COLORS)
7. WHITE GLUE
8. RUBBER CEMENT
9. CRAYONS AND/OR TEMPERA PAINT
10. EASEL BRUSHES
11. WATER CONTAINERS
12. AN ASSORTMENT OF PENCILS

ACTIVITIES:

1. ASSIGN EACH CHILD TO A GROUP ..... THIS
   WILL DIVIDE THE CLASS INTO MANAGEABLE
   UNITS
2. EACH GROUP MUST THEN DIVIDE ONE OF THE
   BUTCHER PAPER SHEETS INTO TEN UNITS
   SOMETHING LIKE A JIG-SAW PUZZLE .....
   OR ..... RATHER THAN THE CONVOLUTED
   LINE FOUND IN SUCH A PUZZLE, A GROUP
   MIGHT ELECT TO USE ALL GEOMETRIC
   PATTERNS (THE IMPORTANT POINT IS THAT
   THE CORRECT NUMBER OF AREAS RESULT AND
   THAT THE YOUNGSTERS HAVE A CHOICE)

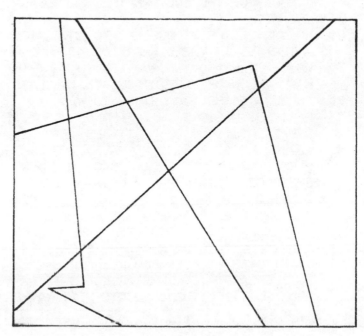

3. THE RESULT OF STEP 2 WILL BE TO FORM
A KIND OF "JIG-SAW" PUZZLE ..... FROM
WHICH EACH CHILD CHOOSES HIS "OWN"
SECTION OF THE "PUZZLE"

4. THE SECTIONS ARE THEN CUT APART AND
LABELED AS TO WHICH IS "UP" AND WHICH
"DOWN"

5. USING HIS SECTION, THE YOUNGSTER THEN
COMPOSES A VISUAL REPRESENTATION (IT
MIGHT BE A DRAWING, A PICTURE, OR A
COLLAGE) USING ANY MATERIAL AND MEDIA
HE CHOOSES, WHICH WILL REPRESENT ONE
CULTURAL AREA (INDIAN, ASIAN, BLACK,
CHICANO, ETC.) ENCOURAGE THE YOUNG-
STERS TO EXPLORE ALTERNATIVE POSSI-
BILITIES ..... THEY MAY WORK IN A
REALISTIC AND REPRESENTATIONAL MANNER
OR THEY MAY ELECT TO WORK WITH THE
SYMBOLS OF THE CULTURE THEY ARE DEAL-
ING WITH.

6. ENCOURAGE THE YOUNGSTERS TO INVESTIGATE
MATERIALS IN THE LIBRARY OR AT HOME
WHICH WILL ADD INFORMATION TO WHAT THEY
MIGHT KNOW OR HAVE DISCUSSED IN CLASS.

7. ENCOURAGE THE YOUNGSTERS TO WORK IN
DESIGNS, DESIGNS IN THE MANNER OF ....
REPRESENTATIONS OF FESTIVALS, ETC.

8. AFTER THE COMPOSITIONS HAVE BEEN COM-
PLETED MOUNT THE SECTIONS ON ANOTHER
SHEET OF BUTCHER PAPER USING WHITE
GLUE TO SECURE THEM IN PLACE .... LET
THE CHILDREN REASSEMBLE THE TOTAL UNIT

9. WITH A HEAVY MARKING PEN, HAVE ONE OF
THE YOUNGSTERS DRAW AROUND EACH SEC-
TION TO SET IT OFF AND REINFORCE THE
PUZZLE BASE ..... WHAT RESULTS IS A
TRUE MULTI-CULTURAL MOSAIC. IT MAY BE

LAMINATED, OR PRESERVED WITH A STRONG
FIXATIF (HAIR SPRAY, COMMERCIAL FIX-
ATIF, OR POLYMER MATTE OR GLOSS MEDIUM
ARE A FEW CHOICES OPEN TO YOU) AND
DISPLAYED IN THE CLASSROOM OR OUT IN
THE CORRIDOR

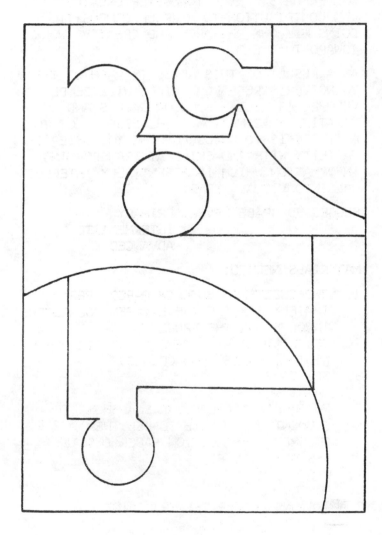

NOTES FOR THE TEACHER

THIS ACTIVITY IS ALWAYS A DELIGHT FOR THE
YOUNGSTERS AND A SURPRISE FOR THE TEACHER
BECAUSE, AT FIRST, REGARDLESS OF THE AGES
OF THE PARTICIPANTS, NO ONE SEEMS ABLE TO
IMAGINE HOW IT WILL ALL TURN OUT SINCE
EACH PERSON IS DOING SOMETHING INDIVIDUAL,
ORIGINAL, AND (HOPEFULLY) QUITE DIFFERENT
WITH HIS PARTICULAR SECTION OF THE TOTAL
COMPOSITIONAL UNIT.

WHEN ALL OF THE INDIVIDUAL PARTS ARE
COMPLETED, FITTED BACK TOGETHER AGAIN, AND
GLUED INTO PLACE, THE FINISHED PRODUCT
DEMONSTRATES THE CONCEPT THAT AMERICA IS
NOT, IN REALITY, A "MELTING POT" WHICH
MAKES ALL CULTURES AND CULTURAL GROUPS
ALIKE, BUT ACTUALLY A "MOSAIC" IN WHICH
CULTURES AND CULTURAL GROUPS EACH CONTRIB-
UTE TO THE OVER-ALL GOOD, WORTH, AND
BEAUTY OF THE WHOLE.

THIS ACTIVITY CAN BE USED AT ANY GRADE
LEVEL WITH A GOOD DEAL OF SUCCESS .....
EVEN EXTENDING INTO A TEACHER IN-SERVICE
PROGRAM.

WHERE IS HOME?

THIS ACTIVITY HAS A THREE-FOLD PURPOSE:
(1) TO ENCOURAGE THE YOUNGSTERS TO RECOG-
NIZE THE FACT THAT ALL LIVING THINGS HAVE
"HOMES," (2) TO BRING ABOUT THE CONCEPT-
UALIZATION THAT THERE ARE A NUMBER OF
DIFFERENT WAYS IN WHICH THE PEOPLE OF DIF-
FERENT CULTURES BUILD THEIR HOMES, AND
(3) TO ENCOURAGE INTEREST IN AND EXPERIENCE
WITH THE SKILLS OF CATAGORIZING AND CLASS-
IFYING.

SUGGESTED GRADE LEVEL: PRIMARY
INTERMEDIATE
ADVANCED

MATERIALS NEEDED:

1. A DICTIONARY
2. AN ENCYCLOPOEDIA
3. PAPER
4. PENCILS OR PENS
5. BLACKBOARD
6. CHALK (WHITE AND ASSORTED COLORS)

ACTIVITIES:

1. EACH YOUNGSTER BEGINS A LISTING OF ALL
OF THE WORDS HE CAN THINK OF WHICH
MIGHT MEAN "HOME"
2. NEXT TO EACH OF THE WORDS ON HIS LIST
HE WRITES THE NAME OF WHO OR WHATEVER
MIGHT LIVE IN THAT "HOME"
3. FROM EACH OF THE INDIVIDUAL LISTS
A MASTER LISTING IS COMPOSED ON THE
BLACKBOARD, THE "HOMES" MIGHT BE IN
WHITE WHILE THE "INHABITANTS" MIGHT
BE IN A DIFFERENT COLOR .....

1. WEB – SPIDER
2. LAIR – TIGER
3. NEST – BIRD/RAT/MOUSE
4. DEN – LION
5. HOLE – MOLE/CHIPMUNK
6. WARREN – RABBIT
7. HUTCH – RABBIT
8. STABLE – HORSE
9. BARN – COW
10. COOP – CHICKEN
11. HILL – ANT
12. TREE – SQUIRREL
13. DAM – BEAVER

..... THE LIST CAN BE ENLARGED FOR AS
LONG AS INTEREST AND INFORMATION CON-
TINUE

5. IN THE SAME MANNER MAKE ANOTHER LIST,
THIS ONE OF WORDS WHICH MEAN "HUMAN
HOMES," ENCOURAGING THE YOUNGSTERS TO
RECOGNIZE THAT SUCH A LISTING MAY
COVER A WIDE RANGE OF GEOGRAPHIC AND
CULTURAL DIFFERENCES
6. NEXT TO EACH WORD ON HIS LIST HE SHOULD
INDICATE EITHER GEOGRAPHIC LOCATION IN
WHICH SUCH A HABITATION IS FOUND OR
THE PARTICULAR CULTURE RESPONSIBLE FOR
ITS CONSTRUCTION
6. FROM EACH LIST COMPOSE A MASTER LIST
ON THE BLACKBOARD .....

1. ADOBE – SOUTHWEST USA
2. HACIENDA – MEXICO
3. CASA – MEXICO
4. TEEPEE – SIOUX INDIAN
5. HOGAN – NAVAHO INDIAN
6. LONG-HOUSE – IROQUOIS INDIAN
7. PUEBLO – SOUTHWEST USA

8. MOUND	–	INDIANS OF THE MISSISSIPPI RIVER BASIN
9. SAMPAN	–	CHINESE
10. GRASS HUT	–	NATIVE AFRICAN
11. STILT HOUSE	–	SOUTHEAST ASIA
12. LOG CABIN	–	EARLY AMERICAN SETTLERS AND SLAVES
13. IGLOO	–	ESKIMO
14. I-E	–	SIMPLE JAPAN-ESE HOUSE
15. YASHIKE	–	COMPLEX JAPAN-ESE HOUSE
16. MOTEL/HOTEL	–	TEMPORARY HOME U.S.A. AND MANY OTHER COUNTRIES
17. TRAILER	–	"
18. MOBILE HOME	–	U.S.A. AND MANY OTHER COUNTRIES
19. APARTMENT	–	"
20. FLAT	–	"
21. CONDOMINIUM	–	"
22. DUPLEX	–	"
23. HOUSEBOAT	–	"
24. TENT	–	"
25. DOME	–	"
26. CAVE	–	EARLY MAN AND ANIMALS
27. SPACE POD	–	?
28. SPACE PLAT-FORM	–	?
29. CASTLE	–	ROYALTY
30. PALACE	–	VERY RICH ROYALTY

..... ENCOURAGE THE YOUNGSTERS TO ADD TO THIS LIST FOR AS LONG AS INTEREST AND INFORMATION CONTINUE

7. WHEN YOU HAVE COLLECTED A REASONABLE (THAT IS UP TO YOU) LISTING OF TERMS BEGIN TO CLASSIFY THEM IN AS MANY WAYS AS POSSIBLE ..... FOR EXAMPLE, LISTING THE HOMES ANIMALS, BIRDS, AND INSECTS CONSTRUCT FOR THEMSELVES COMPARED TO THE HOMES PEOPLE HAVE MADE FOR ANIMALS, BIRDS, AND INSECTS .....

HOMES ANIMALS MAKE FOR THEMSELVES	HOMES MAN HAS MADE FOR ANIMALS
CAVE	BARN
DEN	HUTCH
NEST	STABLE
HILL	DOG HOUSE
HIVE	HIVE
WEB	AVIARY

..... WHICH WILL PROVIDE ONE IDEA OF THE RELATIONSHIP BETWEEN "ABODES" AND THEN GO ON TO A LISTING OF THE KINDS OF HOMES MAN HAS MADE FOR HIMSELF IN THE PAST, THOSE HE MAKES IN THE PRESENT, AND THOSE HE WILL MAKE IN THE FUTURE .....

HOMES THAT MAN HAS MADE/WILL MAKE FOR HIMSELF

PAST	PRESENT	FUTURE
CAVE	HOUSE	DOME
PUEBLO	CONDOMINIUM	HABITAT

..... WHICH ENCOURAGES COMPARITIVE THINKING AND CONCEPTUALIZATION OF A TIME SPAN

NOTES FOR THE TEACHER

THE MOST IMPORTANT POINT IN THIS ACTIVITY IS THE CONCEPT THAT ALL LIVING THINGS NEED SOME KIND OF SHELTER; FROM THE COMPLEX, MECHANIZED HABITATS THAT HUMAN BEINGS NEED AND SEEM TO OCCUPY ..... TO THE COOL SHADE OF A ROCK WHICH MIGHT SHELTER SOME DENIZEN OF THE DESERT. INHERENT IN THESE CONSID-ERATIONS IS THE OPPORTUNITY TO DEVELOP AWARENESS AND RECOGNITION OF THE FACTORS OF PERSONAL SPACE, TERRATORIAL IMPERATIVE, AND PRIVACY.

FROM SUCH CONSIDERATIONS COME THE UNDER-STANDING OF THE DIFFERENCES BETWEEN DETACHED HOUSES, CONDOMINIUMS, CLUSTER HOUSING, TRACT DEVELOPMENT, TENEMENT LIVING, AND THE LIKE ..... ALL OF THE WAYS OF BUILDING WHICH PROVIDE DIFFERING DEGREES OF PRIVACY AND THE SAFETY OF LIVING IN SETTLEMENT SITUATIONS.

ALSO ..... THERE IS THE CONSIDERATION OF THE "PORTABLE HOME" ..... FOR EXAMPLE, ALL EXOSKELETAL ANIMALS CARRY THEIR SHELTER (HOMES) ALONG WITH THEM (SNAILS, CRABS, ARMADILLOS, TURTLES.) MAN HAS DEVELOPED SUCH A SYSTEM WITH THE ADVENT OF THE MOBILE HOME OR RECREATIONAL VEHICLE WHICH CAN BE AS SIMPLE AS A VAN WITH A MATTRESS ON ITS FLOOR, OR AS COMPLEX AS THE MOST EXPENSIVE, SELF-CONTAINED, TRAVEL HOME. LIKE SUCH ANIMALS, MAN HAS DEVELOPED A SHELTER SYSTEM WHICH SUITS HIS GEOGRAPHIC LOCATION AND/OR HIS PHYSICAL AND SOCIAL NEEDS.

IN ALL CASES, THE CONCEPTS OF SHELTER AND SAFETY, LARGE OR SMALL, ARE OF PRIME IMPORTANCE.

THIS ACTIVITY MIGHT DEVELOP INTO A UNIT ON HOMES AROUND THE WORLD WITH CORRELATIVE FACTORS IN ECONOMICS (ESPECIALLY APPLIC-ABLE TO/FOR THE ADVANCED LEVELS) DEALING WITH THE CONCEPTS OF REAL ESTATE, OWNER-SHIP, TAXES, MARKETING, ETC.

THE DEPTH TO WHICH YOU GO WITH THIS ACTIVITY DEPENDS ENTIRELY UPON YOU, YOUR COMMITTMENT, AND THE AGE LEVEL OF YOUR YOUNGSTERS.

TEACHER'S NOTES

CHUKEN HACHIKO

THIS ACTIVITY IS, PERHAPS, ONE OF THE LEAST INVOLVED OF ANY ACTIVITIES IN THIS BOOK, YET, IT MAY HAVE ONE OF THE MOST TELLING EFFECTS UPON YOUR YOUNGSTERS.

THE STORY IS TRUE, YET YOU NEED NOT SHARE THAT FACT WITH THE YOUNGSTERS AT FIRST. CHUKEN HACHIKO REPRESENTS FAITHFULLLNESS TO THE JAPANESE, AN ATTRIBUTE AS IMPORTANT TO THE JAPANESE TODAY, AS IT WAS SO MANY YEARS AGO.

THE STORY IS MEANT FOR YOU TO TELL TO YOUR YOUNGSTERS, REGARDLESS OF HOW OLD THEY MAY BE. IF THEY ARE PRIMARY LEVEL, THE STORY ALONE WILL BE QUITE INVOLVED ENOUGH, IF THEY ARE INTERMEDIATE AND ADVANCED LEVELS IT MIGHT BE WISE TO INCLUDE SOME OF THE INFORMATION YOU WILL FIND IN THE FOLLOWING, NOTES FOR THE TEACHER.

THIS ACTIVITY, BETTER THAN ANY OTHER, MAY FORGE THE LINK BETWEEN ILLUSION AND REALITY FOR YOUR YOUNGSTERS.

SUGGESTED GRADE LEVEL: PRIMARY
                       INTERMEDIATE
                       ADVANCED

MATERIALS NEEDED:

1. SEAT THE YOUNGSTERS COMFORTABLY SO THAT THEY WILL PAY CAREFUL ATTENTION
2. THE STORY WHICH FOLLOWS
3. AN EXPRESSIVE READING VOICE

ACTIVITIES:

1. SEAT THE YOUNGSTERS COMFORTABLY
2. READ THE FOLLOWING STORY .....

ONCE UPON A TIME, DURING THE WAR BETWEEN THE UNITED STATES AND JAPAN, IN A SMALL VILLAGE CALLED SHIBUYA THERE LIVED A YOUNG MAN CALLED YOSHIAKI. HE LIVED ALL ALONE ON A SMALL PATCH OF GROUND WHICH PRODUCED RICE AND OTHER VEGETABLES WHICH KEPT HIM AND HIS LITTLE DOG, CHUKEN HACHIKO, FROM BEING HUNGRY AND WHICH ALSO PRODUCED A LITTLE OVER THEIR NEEDS WHICH COULD BE SOLD IN THE MARKET NEAR THE RAILROAD STATION.

IT WAS NOT AN EASY LIFE, BUT "AKI," AS HIS FRIENDS CALLED HIM, WAS A CHEERFUL PERSON WITH A READY SMILE AND A BRIGHT HELLO FOR EVERYONE. HE AND THE LITTLE DOG WERE A WELCOME AND FAMILIAR SIGHT AS THEY WENT THROUGH THE VILLAGE, AKI WITH A CHEERY HELLO AND A BRIGHT WAVE AND THE LITTLE DOG TRIPPING ALONG BESIDE HIM, TAIL WAGGING LETTING OUT AN OCCASSIONAL "YIP" BY WAY OF GREETING HIMSELF.

AS THE WAR PROGRESSED IN THE EARLY 1940S AND THE ARMY NEEDED MORE AND MORE FOOD TO FEED THEIR MEN, IT BECAME DIFFICULT TO FIND ENOUGH FOOD IN THE VILLAGE TO MEET EVERYONE'S NEEDS BUT AKI MANAGED TO KEEP HIMSELF AND HIS LITTLE DOG RELATIVELY COMFORTABLE AND GIVE WHAT WAS REQUIRED OF HIM TO THE ARMY AND EVEN FIND A LITTLE TO SHARE WITH THOSE IN THE VILLAGE LESS FORTUNATE.

AS THE WAR WENT ON AND JAPAN'S FORTUNES WENT WRONG, ALL OF THE YOUNG MEN

WERE CALLED UP FOR DUTY, EVEN THOSE LIKE
AKI WHO WERE ENGAGED IN WORK WHICH HELPED
THE MILITARY.

ALL OF THE YOUNG MEN IN THE VILLAGE WERE
CALLED UP AND SLOWLY EACH TOOK THE TRAIN
FROM SHIBUYA WHICH WOULD TAKE THEM TO THE
MILITARY ACADEMY AT SOBA DAI, TO THE NORTH
OF TOKYO. AKI TRIED DESPERATELY TO FIND
A FAMILY WHICH WOULD TAKE CARE OF LITTLE
CHUKEN HACHIKO AND FINALLY TWO OLD PEOPLE
AGREED TO CARE FOR THE LITTLE DOG, AND
AKI PACKED HIS FEW BELONGINGS AND SAYING
GOODBYE TO THE LITTLE DOG HE WALKED TO THE
STATION.

LITTLE CHUKEN HACHIKO WAS TERRIBLY UPSET.
HE KNEW HIS MASTER WAS GOING AWAY, HE KNEW
THE OLD PEOPLE WERE TO BE HIS NEW MASTERS
UNTIL AKI RETURNED. HE DIDN'T WANT TO STAY
WITH THEM EVEN THOUGH HE KNEW THEY WOULD
BE GOOD TO HIM. HE BROKE THROUGH THE ROPE
WITH WHICH AKI HAD TIED HIM BEFORE HE LEFT
AND RACED TO FOLLOW AKI, REACHING SHIBUYA
JUST AS THE TRAIN CARRYING AKI TO SOBA DAI
WAS LEAVING THE STATION. HE RACED ALONG
SIDE THE TRAIN, BARKING AND BARKING UNTIL
AKI CAME TO THE DOOR AND WAVED TO HIM
SHOUTING THAT HE MUST GO BACK. THE LITTLE
DOG DIDN'T WANT TO GO BACK BUT THE TRAIN
WAS MOVING SO QUICKLY, HE COULDN'T KEEP
UP SO HE STOPPED, SAT ON THE SIDE OF THE
RAILROAD BED AND CRIED UNTIL THE TRAIN WAS
WAY OUT OF SIGHT.

LATER, HE SLOWLY WALKED BACK TO THE TRAIN
STATION IN THE CENTER OF SHIBUYA, SAT
DOWN IN FRONT OF THE STATION AND WAITED
FOR AKI TO COME HOME.

HE WAITED FOR A LONG, LONG TIME. HE
KNEW IT WAS PAST WHEN HE WAS USED TO
EATING BUT HE WOULDN'T LEAVE THAT SPOT.
THE OLD PEOPLE AKI HAD ENTRUSTED WITH
HIS LITTLE FRIEND CAME LOOKING FOR HIM
AND WANTED TO TAKE HIM HOME BUT HE
WOULDN'T MOVE. THE OLD MAN TRIED TO
CARRY HIM HOME BUT LITTLE CHUKEN
HACHIKO WAS TOO HEAVY TO CARRY FOR VERY
LONG FOR THE OLD MAN AND EACH TIME HE
HAD TO PUT THE LITTLE DOG DOWN, CHUKEN
HACHIKO WOULD RUN BACK TO THE STATION
AND THE PLACE HE DECIDED TO WAIT FOR
AKI.

SOON THE OLD PEOPLE GAVE UP TRYING TO
GET THE LITTLE DOG HOME AND INSTEAD
BROUGHT FOOD TO HIM AT THE STATION.
SOON THE LITTLE DOG BECAME A FAMILIAR
SIGHT TO EVERYONE IN THE VILLAGE AS HE
WAS ALWAYS IN THE SAME SPOT NO MATTER
WHAT THE WEATHER, NEVER LEAVING IT
EXCEPT FOR IMPORTANT MATTERS WHICH HAD
TO BE ATTENDED TO.

CHUKEN HACHIKO SPENT MANY MONTHS IN
THAT SPOT WAITING FOR AKI TO COME HOME
AND SOON THE OLD PEOPLE AKI HAD EN-
TRUSTED HIM WITH WERE NO LONGER ABLE
TO BRING FOOD TO THE LITTLE DOG AND IT
LOOKED AS IF HE WOULD STARVE, FOR HE
WOULD NOT LEAVE THAT SPOT. HE HAD TO
BE THERE FOR WHEN AKI CAME HOME AND
LITTLE CHUKEN HACHIKO KNEW THAT AKI
WOULD COME HOME. ALL THE VILLAGERS
TALKED ABOUT HOW LOYAL THE LITTLE DOG
WAS. THE CHILDREN ALL KNEW HIM AND
THEY BROUGHT HIM SCRAPS OF FOOD THEY

HAD SAVED AND BUILT A LITTLE LEAN-TO OF
BAMBOO AND LEAVES OVER HIM TO PROTECT HIM
FROM THE RAIN AND SNOW.

CHUKEN HACHIKO WAITED FOR AKI TO COME HOME
FOR A LONG TIME, BUT THE WEATHER WAS TOO
MUCH FOR THE LITTLE DOG AND IT WASN'T VERY
LONG BEFORE HE DIED, STILL WAITING FOR AKI
TO COME HOME ..... BUT EVEN AFTER THE
LITTLE DOG DIED, AKI NEVER RETURNED.

THE JAPANESE CHILDREN OF THE VILLAGE WERE
TOLD THAT SINCE AKI COULDN'T COME HOME TO
CHUKEN HACHIKO, THE LITTLE DOG WENT TO
WHERE AKI WAS.

TODAY, MANY YEARS LATER, IN THAT VERY SPOT
WHERE THE LITTLE DOG WAITED FOR AKI, THE
PEOPLE OF SHIBUYA HAVE PLACED A STATUE OF
THE LITTLE DOG AND IT SITS RIGHT IN FRONT
OF WHERE THE SHIBUYA RAILROAD STATION AND
THE HUGE TOKYO DEPARTMENT STORE JOIN EACH
OTHER.

TODAY THE STATUE IS ALMOST A FOLK LEGEND
TO THE YOUNG PEOPLE OF JAPAN ..... IT
SYMBOLIZES FAITHFULNESS AND LOYALTY TO
THE JAPANESE, AND CHUKEN HACHIKO'S STATUE
IS A FAVORITE MEETING PLACE FOR PEOPLE
FROM ALL OVER THE AREA.

NOTES FOR THE TEACHER

EACH COUNTRY, EACH CULTURE, HAS "STORIES" WHICH SOME CALL "TALES," OTHERS CALL "YARNS," AND STILL OTHERS CALL "MYTHS." IN SOME INSTANCES SUCH STORIES ARE BASED ON FACT AND ARE ESSENTIALLY TRUE; BUT MOST OFTEN THEY ARE THE PRODUCT OF THE PREGNANT IMAGINATION OF A POET, TROUBADOUR, STORY-TELLER, OR WRITER. WHATEVER THE CASE, ALL SUCH STORIES, IN ADDITION TO BEING WON-DERFULLY ENTERTAINING IN A PURELY LITERARY WAY, ARE VERY STRONG IN THEIR INDICATION OF A NATIONAL TONE, AN INDICATION OF THE WAY A CULTURE VIEWS ITSELF AND THE WORLD.

IN LIBRARIES ALL OVER THE WORLD THERE ARE WONDERFUL BOOKS TEEMING WITH STORIES CON-CERNING VARIOUS CULTURAL HERITAGES, FOLK TALES, MYTHOLOGY, AND THE LIKE WHICH CON-CERN EACH CULTURE AND SUCH BOOKS ARE TREASURE TROVES FOR TEACHERS TO SHARE WITH THEIR YOUNGSTERS. IN ADDITION, THERE ARE TRUE STORIES WHICH, OFTEN, WILL POINT VERY STRONGLY TO THE HUMANISTIC QUALITIES OF A PEOPLE AND EMPHASIZE OUR SIMILARITIES AS WELL AS OUR DIFFERENCES.

IN TRAVELING THROUGH THE ORIENT NOT LONG AGO THE AUTHORS SPENT SOME TIME IN JAPAN AND IN TRAVELING THROUGH ONE OF THE LARGEST CITIES IN THE WORLD, TOKYO, WE FOUND OURSELVES IN A SECTION OF TOKYO CALLED SHIBUYA. THIS SECTION OCCUPIES AN AREA COMPARABLE TO THAT OF SAN FRAN-CISCO, CALIFORNIA AND HOUSES ALMOST TWICE THE POPULATION. AS IN MOST SUBCITIES IN JAPAN, THE CENTER OF THE UNIT IS THE RAILROAD STATION AROUND WHICH THE SECTION GROWS.

SHIBUYA RAILROAD STATION IS BOTH A TERMINAL FOR THE LOCAL RAPID TRANSIT WHICH TRAVERSES TOKYO AND IS ALSO A MAJOR TERMINAL FOR THE TRAINS WHICH TRAVERSE THE COUNTRY. IT IS A BUILDING WHICH STANDS EIGHT STORIES TALL AND DIRECTLY ADJOINS THE HUGE TOKYO DEPART-MENT STORE AND HANDLES RAIL TRAFFIC THAT IS STAGGERING. THE AVERAGE DAILY PASSENGER TRAFFIC IS SOMETHING AROUND TWO HUNDRED THOUSAND PEOPLE.

DIRECTLY IN FRONT OF THE MAIN ENTRANCE TO SHIBUYA STATION IS A GRANITE PEDESTAL SOME THREE FEET HIGH ON TOP OF WHICH IS SEATED AN ADORABLE LITTLE DOG, CHUKEN HACHIKO, THE SUBJECT OF THE PRECEEDING STORY. THERE ARE NO WORDS TO DESCRIBE THE CRUSH OF LITERALLY THOUSANDS OF PEOPLE WHO COME THROUGH THE DOORS AND ALL ACROSS THE PLAZA AND MUST PASS THE LITTLE DOG, YET NO MATTER WHAT THE RUSH, HOW MANY PEOPLE IN THE CRUSH EVERYONE HAS AN AFFECTIONATE GLANCE FOR THE LITTLE STATUE ..... HE REPRESENTS TO THEM ALL THAT IS THE BEST IN LIFE.

THERE IS ONLY ONE OTHER STATUE IN THE WORLD THAT WE KNOW OF THAT ELICITS THAT KIND OF WARM, FRIENDLY, AND COMFORTABLE RESPONSE AND THAT IS THE LITTLE MERMAID OF HAN CHRISTIAN ANDERSON FAME WHICH RESTS ATOP A ROCK IN COPENHAGEN HARBOR.

PERHAPS HERE IS A PLACE TO TALK WITH THE CHILDREN ABOUT THAT SPECIAL SOMETHING WHICH MEANS THE MOST TO THEM ..... THE STORY OF THE LITTLE DOG WAS TOLD TO US BY A VERY OLD LADY WHO SAW US PUZZLING OVER THE JAPANESE AND WANTED TO SHARE THE BEAUTY WITH US.

TEACHER'S NOTES

CROSSWORD PUZZLE

THIS ACTIVITY IS DESIGNED TO ENCOURAGE THE LANGUAGE ARTS POTENTIALS WITHIN THE MULTI-CULTURAL STUDIES SITUATION, USING WORDS WHICH, IN LARGE MEASURE, COME FROM AN IN-CREASING AWARENESS OF OTHER PEOPLE AND THEIR CULTURES.

SUGGESTED GRADE LEVEL: INTERMEDIATE
                                ADVANCED

MATERIALS NEEDED:

1. PUZZLE(S)
2. PENCILS
3. DICTIONARIES

ACTIVITIES:

1. DETAIL A BRIEF EXPLANATION OF HOW A CROSSWORD PUZZLE WORKS (FOR THOSE WHO MAY NOT HAVE WORKED ONE BEFORE)
2. GO TO IT!

ACROSS

1. THIRD NOTE ON THE MUSICAL SCALE
3. ROMAN NUMERAL FOR NUMBER SIX (6)
5. NATURAL FIBRE GROWN IN THE SOUTH
11. THE BOTH OF US
13. JAPANESE STAPLE FOOD ..... RAW FISH ON RICE BALLS
20. UNREFINED MINERAL
23. FORMER
26. ORIENTAL PEOPLE FROM CONTINENT
32. AND
35. A UNIT OF MEASURE IN ELECTRICITY
38. NATIVE AMERICANS
45. ROMAN NUMERAL FOR NUMBER TEN (10)
47. INDIAN HABITATION FOUND IN THE SOUTHWEST
54. ABREVIATION FOR LONG ISLAND
57. THING, PART, ANIMAL, THAT WHICH IS SPOKEN ABOUT
59. GREEK LETTER
62. THE OBJECTIVE CASE OF "WE"
64. A LARGE MEXICAN HOUSE
72. ROMAN NUMERAL FOR THE NUMBER ONE HUNDRED (100)
73. A COUNTRY SOUTH OF THE BORDER
80. A SOUND OF GREAT SPEED
84. THE PERSON OR THING WHICH IS PRESENT
88. THE MACHINE WHICH PACKAGES COTTON INTO THE UNITS BY WHICH IT IS SOLD
93. A RIVER IN NORTHERN ITALY
96. A SOUND OF EXCLAMATION!
98. OTHER THAN, DIFFERENT
102. CONTRACTION FOR "HE IS"
106. COLLOQUIALISM FOR FATHER
108. ANY, ONE, EACH
109. PREJUDICES
115. SECOND NOTE ON THE MUSICAL SCALE
117. A CHINESE "WATER PERSON'S HOME"
123. EACH
125. ROMAN NUMERAL FOR NUMBER ONE HUNDRED (100)
126. ROMAN NUMERAL FOR NUMBER ONE THOUSAND (1,000)
127. SPEAKER OR WRITER, HIMSELF
128. ACTIVITIES
134. SMALL, WINGLESS PARASITES
138. THE FIFTH LETTER OF THE ALPHABET

DOWN

1. LEGENDARY LAND FROM THE STORIES OF JOHN CARTER OF BARSOOM
2. THIRD PERSON SINGULAR, PRESENT INDICATIVE OF "BE"
3. AN ITALIAN AVENUE
4. FIRST PERSON SINGULAR
5. ROMAN NUMERAL FOR NUMBER ONE HUNDRED (100)
6. COVERING MANY THINGS AT ONCE
8. IN THE DIRECTION OF
9. ROCK, SAND, OR DIRT CONTAINING SOME METAL (PLURAL)
10. A TRAP OR SNARE TO CATCH FISH ORIGINATED BY THE JAPANESE
11. A SPIDER'S HOME
12. FOR EXAMPLE, AS EXAMPLE
13. HALT!
18. BREAKING THE LAW OF GOD
25. THE UPPER SURFACE
27. AN INDIAN TRIBE FOUND ON THE MIDDLE PLAINS
28. OPPOSITE FROM "IN"
29. INCREASE
31. FRENCH WORD MEANING ROOM

36. A PEN FOR RABBITS
37. ITALIAN WORD FOR MY OR MINE
43. A DEGREE OF BEING PLEASANT, KIND, WARM, AND FRIENDLY
45. ROMAN NUMERAL FOR NUMBER TEN (10)
46. SMALL PIECES OF PAPER WITH STICKY BACKS PLACED ON LETTERS OR PARCELS
50. TRAMPS, DISREPUTABLE PEOPLE
51. ROMAN NUMERAL FOR NUMBER FIFTY (50)
56. AN INDIAN TRIBE FOUND IN THE STATES OF IDAHO AND MONTANA
57. TWO WORDS SIGNIFYING AFFIRMATIVE INTENT OR ACTION
63. BROTHERS AND SISTERS
64. HOLLOW PLACES IN SOMETHING SOLID
67. SPEAKER OR PERSON, HIMSELF
69. A LOOP WITH A SLIP KNOT WHICH TIGHTENS AS THE STRING OR ROPE IS PULLED
70. TO PERFORM, TO MAKE
84. A TOY THAT SPINS ON A POINT
86. ABBREVIATION FOR ISRAEL
98. PRIME MINISTER OF ISRAEL, ABBA ----
107. IN THE SAME WAY THAT .....
108. LATIN FORM FOR LOVE
113. A LONG SLIPPERY FISH SHAPED LIKE A SNAKE
114. A MONKEY FOUND IN THE PLAINS OF CENTRAL AFRICA
118. COLLOQUIALISM MEANING ADVERTISEMENT
120. ABBREVIATION FOR THE PHILLIPINES
126. THE OBJECTIVE OR ACCUSATIVE CASE OF I

NOTES FOR THE TEACHER

THIS CROSSWORD PUZZLE WAS CREATED AND DRAFTED IN A LITTLE UNDER THREE HOURS. THERE IS NO DOUBT THAT WITH MORE TIME A FAR BETTER PUZZLE WOULD BE PRODUCED BUT OUR INTENT IS TO DEMONSTRATE THAT SUCH PUZZLES ARE NOT DIFFICULT TO CONSTRUCT AND THAT THEY DON'T NECESSARILY HAVE TO LOOK LIKE THE NEW YORK TIMES SUNDAY BRAINBUSTER. WE WANT TO ENCOURAGE YOU AND YOUR YOUNGSTERS TO DEVELOP YOUR OWN PUZZLES WHICH WILL ALLOW YOU (THE TEACHER) TO DISCOVER THE EXTENT OF YOUR YOUNGSTER'S INFORMATION AND HOW ABLE EACH IS IN EXPRESSING SUCH INFORMATION IN A RELATIVELY DIFFERENT FORMAT.

PERHAPS THE MOST DIFFICULT PART OF TEACHING IS LEARNING WHETHER OR NOT YOUR YOUNGSTERS HAVE VIABLE "RETRIEVAL" SYSTEMS AND WHETHER THESE SYSTEMS ARE CAPABLE OF TRANSFERRING INFORMATION AS REQUIRED.

THERE IS NOTHING BETTER THAN A CROSSWORD PUZZLE TO GAIN EXPERIENCE IN AND PRACTICE WITH REFERENCE AND CROSS-REFERENCE FACTOR SITUATIONS. HERE IS A NON-THREATENING TEST BUT THE TESTING IS COUCHED IN A "GAME PLAYING SITUATION" WHICH WILL OFTEN UNLOCK SKILL AND EXPERTISE WHICH UNDER THE TRADITIONAL TESTING PATTERNS ARE BLOCKED.

AS A CORRELARY TO SUCH AN ACTIVITY, ANY WORD GAME SUCH AS SCRABBLE, ETC. IS VERY DESIRABLE.

IT WILL ALSO BE NECESSARY FOR YOU TO DIS-
CARD EVERY RULE YOU MAY HAVE LEARNED AS
TO THE VOCABULARY LIMITATIONS YOUR GRADE
LEVEL YOUNGSTERS MAY HAVE. IT IS THE
AUTHOR'S EXPERIENCE THAT THE ONLY LIMIT-
ATIONS ON A YOUNGSTER'S VOCABULARY ARE
THOSE ARBITRARILY APPLIED BY TEXTBOOK
WRITERS AND THOSE EDUCATORS WHO HAVE BEEN
AROUND "TOO LONG!"

YOU WILL BE AMAZED, AND VERY PLEASANTLY
SURPRISED, TO DISCOVER THAT EVEN THE MOST
OBSCURE WORDS CAN BE SEARCHED OUT BY
YOUNGSTERS HAVING FUN DOING THE DETECTIVE
WORK ..... THOUGH YOU WILL HAVE TO WATCH
CAREFULLY AND BE ABLE TO PROVIDE THE HELP
THEY MAY NEED TO "RESEARCH" THE WORDS AT
THE RIGHT TIME.

THE CROSSWORD PUZZLE WE HAVE PROVIDED IS
ONLY ONE OF MANY, MANY POSSIBILITIES WHICH
YOU AND YOUR YOUNGSTERS CAN DEVISE .....
YOU MIGHT DUPLICATE THE ONE WE HAVE PRO-
VIDED AS A START AND BUILD YOUR "ARSENAL"
FROM THERE.

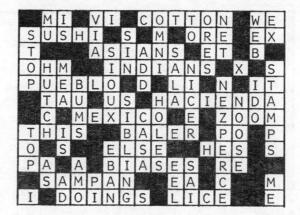

YUKATA

HOPI COAT

MAKING A JAPANESE YUKATA (KIMONO)

PEOPLE WEAR CLOTHES FOR A WIDE VARIETY OF DIFFERENT REASONS; BUT THERE ARE TWO WHICH SEEM TO BE BASIC ..... (1) PROTECTION AGAINST THE ELEMENTS, INSECTS, AND PLANTS WHICH CAN MAKE THE BODY EXTREMELY UNCOMFORTABLE, AND (2) AS DECORATIVE BODY WRAPPING WHICH IS, OFTENTIMES, A STATEMENT OR SIGN OF RANK OR STATUS.

THE DIFFERENCES AMONG CLOTHING PATTERNS, MATERIALS, AND CONSTRUCTION IS, THEREFORE, LARGELY A RESULT OF GEOGRAPHIC AND/OR SOCIOLOGIC INFLUENCE AS WELL AS THAT OF PRACTICALITY.

THE FOLLOWING ATTEMPTS TO PROVIDE A BASIC INTRODUCTION TO CLOTHING DESIGN, CONSTRUCTION, AND DECORATION.

SUGGESTED GRADE LEVEL: INTERMEDIATE
                                    ADVANCED

MATERIALS NEEDED:

1. UNBLEACHED MUSLIN* (TWO YARDS FOR EACH STUDENT SHOULD LEAVE ENOUGH FOR A BELT)
2. YARDSTICK(S)
3. PENCILS
4. SCISSORS
5. FABRIC GLUE
6. INDIA INK
7. EASEL BRUSHES

* MUSLIN IS USUALLY SOLD IN 48" WIDTHS AND DIRECTIONS FOR THIS ACTIVITY ARE BASED UPON SUCH WIDTHS, HOWEVER, IF ONLY 36" WIDTHS ARE AVAILABLE, SLIGHT ADJUSTMENTS WILL PERMIT THE ACTIVITY TO WORK.

ACTIVITIES:

1. EACH OF THE YOUNGSTERS MEASURES OFF TWO YARDS OF FABRIC
2. YARDAGE IS THEN FOLDED IN HALF KEEPING THE FOLD AT THE TOP; AND THEN FOLDED IN HALF FROM THE OPPOSITE DIRECTION KEEPING THAT FOLD AT THE RIGHT .....

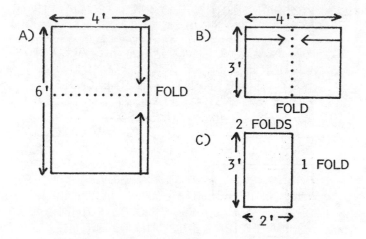

3. THE FOLLOWING STEPS ARE TO BE CARRIED OUT KEEPING THE FABRIC FOLDED AS A UNIT AS IN STEP 2C
4. FROM THE TWO FOLDS AT THE TOP MEASURE DOWN 16" AND RULE A LINE ACROSS THE FABRIC
5. FROM THE FOLD AT THE RIGHT MEASURE ACROSS 12" AND RULE A LINE DOWN THE LENGTH OF THE FABRIC
6. REPEAT STEPS 4 AND 5 ON THE OPPOSITE SURFACE OF THE UNIT KEEPING IN MIND THAT FOR STEP 5, THE SINGLE FOLD WILL BE AT THE LEFT AND THE MEASURING MUST START AT THE FOLD

7. OPEN THE UNIT UP HALF WAY AS IN STEP 2B
8. CUT THE SHADED AREAS OUT AND PUT ASIDE FOR LATER USE .....

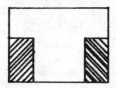

9. YOU NOW HAVE A MODIFIED T SHAPED UNIT WITH THE BASE OF THE T FORMING THE BODY OF THE YUKATA AND THE CROSS PIECE EXTENSIONS FORMING THE SLEEVES
10. MEASURE UP FROM UNDER BODY AND ARM JUNCTURE 6" AND CUT, AS INDICATED BY BROKEN LINES IN DIAGRAM BELOW .....

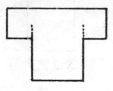

11. MEASURE HALF WAY ACROSS THE WIDTH OF THE BODY AND CUT AN OPENING FROM THE BASE TO THE FOLD <u>BUT CUTTING ONLY ONE PIECE OF FABRIC</u> AS INDICATED BY THE BROKEN LINE IN THE DIAGRAM BELOW

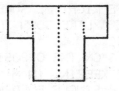

12. OPEN THE ENTIRE PIECE OF FABRIC UP AND IT WILL LOOK LIKE THE DIAGRAM BELOW .....

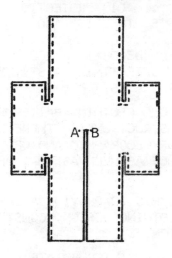

13. YOU MAY FIND IT NECESSARY TO MAKE SMALL CUTS AT POINTS A AND B (APPROXIMATELY 1" OR 2")
14. SQUEEZE A NARROW CHANEL OF FABRIC GLUE ALONG SEAMS AS INDICATED BY BROKEN LINE IN DIAGRAM AND FOLD AND BOND SEAMS HOLDING THEM IN PLACE WITH PINS OR PAPER CLIPS UNTIL GLUE IS DRY
15. TAKE EACH OF THE PIECES YOU PUT ASIDE FROM STEP 8 AND PLACE THEM END TO END SLIGHTLY OVERLAPPING AND GLUE TOGETHER WITH FABRIC GLUE ..... THIS WILL FORM A MODIFIED OBI OR BELT
16. ONCE GLUE HAS HAD TIME TO DRY, TRY THE YUKATA ON AND SEE HOW IT FITS ..... REALIZING THAT IT IS SUPPOSED TO BE QUITE LOOSE

17. ONCE THE YUKATA IS READY TO BE WORN
THE YOUNGSTERS MIGHT CONSIDER THE
DECORATION WHICH IS POSSIBLE, AT FIRST
ON NEWSPRINT PAPER USING INDIA INK AND
BRUSH WORKING THROUGH BAMBOO MOTIFS
AND FLOWERS, ETC.

18. ONCE A DESIGN MOTIF HAS BEEN DECIDED
UPON, USING WATERPROOF INDIA INK AND
EASEL BRUSH, THE SAME DECORATION MAY
BE APPLIED DIRECTLY TO THE YUKATA .....
TAKING CARE THAT THE SECTION OF FABRIC
TO BE PAINTED UPON IS STRETCHED FAIRLY
SECURELY AND BEING SURE THAT A NEWS-
PAPER OR NEWSPRINT PAD BACKS THAT PART
OF THE FABRIC TO BE PAINTED ON AS THE
INK WILL SOAK THROUGH QUITE RAPIDLY
AND DRY ALMOST AT ONCE.

19. WATERFAST FELT TIP PENS MAY ALSO BE
SUCCESSFULLY USED.

NOTES FOR THE TEACHER

THE YUKATA (U-KAH-TUH) IS A COTTON KIMONO
WHICH IS THE "ALL PURPOSE" GARMENT FOR
MANY JAPANESE, ESPECIALLY THOSE WHO LIVE
OUTSIDE OF THE LARGE METROPOLITAN AREAS.

THE DESIGN IS PURELY FUNCTIONAL IN ITS
WRAPAROUND FASHION WHICH ALLOWS ONE SIZE
TO FIT ALMOST EVERYONE. WHEN WRAPPED
AROUND, THERE IS A DOUBLE LAYER OF FABRIC
PROTECTING THE WEARER IN FRONT, AND THE
BELT OR "OBI" SECURES THE GARMENT AND
ALLOWS FOR THE LENGTH TO BE MODIFIED FROM
FULL LENGTH TO KNEE LENGTH WHICH WILL
ACOMMODATE PUDDLES, STREAMS, AND OTHER
OBSTACLES. THE FLOWING SLEEVES ARE MARVELS
OF PRACTICALITY ACOMMODATING WHAT WE WEST-
ERNERS CONSIGN TO POCKETS AND HANDBAGS.

FOR THE JAPANESE, THE YUKATA IS AN INDIS-
PENSIBLE ITEM, WORN AFTER BATHING, OFTEN
AS A NIGHTDRESS OR PAJAMAS, AND, ESPEC-
IALLY IN THE COUNTRYSIDE, AS THE "ALL
PURPOSE" GARMENT FOR WORK AND RELAXATION.

THE YUKATA IS A COMFORTABLE, WARM, FRE-
QUENTLY QUITE BEAUTIFUL AND EXCEEDINGLY
PRACTICAL ITEM AND, AS AN INTRODUCTION TO
THE CUSTOMS INVOLVED IN DRESS IN JAPAN,
WHICH ULTIMATELY LEADS TO THE KIMONO AND
CEREMONIAL DRESS, THIS ACTIVITY PROVIDES
LIMITLESS POSSIBILITIES.

TEACHER'S NOTES

OUR LAND, OUR LAND

A THOUSAND THOUSAND YEARS OR MORE
OUR FATHERS STOOD AMONG THE PINES.
THE LAND GAVE, WE GAVE IN WORSHIP.
THANKFUL, REVERENT, IN AWE WE STOOD.
NURTURED, NOURISHED BY OUR BROTHER
    PLANTS,
OUR SISTER TREES;
SAGE, PINE, WILLOWS ALL GAVE, WE
    RETURNED.
IN HARMONY WE LIVED, BROTHER
    CREATURES.
WE WERE ONE IN OUR LAND.
THE LAND AND ITS
BOUNTY WERE ALL
FOR IT BROUGHT US ALL.

THEN, IN A BLAZING MOMENT
A SCOURGE AROSE FROM THE EAST,
FROM THE RISING SUN
A RAVAGE FROM AFAR.
THE LAND YIELDED, TREES FELL,
WATERS CLOUDED, OUR BROTHER ANIMALS
WEPT.
THE AGES WERE DISTURBED,
CRIED OUT, WERE WOUNDED
IN THEIR TIMELESSNESS.
FOR US THE LAND PROVIDED
NOW IT IS LAID BARREN
BEFORE THE FIERCE PALE ONES.

THE LAND IS PATCHWORK NOW
DIVIDED UP, SECTIONED OFF,
PARCELED OUT, CRISSCROSSED.
BUT IS IT NOT OUR LAND,
GOD'S LAND, THE LAND'S LAND?
RESPECT, REVERENCE, WORSHIP ARE
    GONE

FROM HERE.
WE LIVED HERE. WE WERE IT,
IT WAS US. NO MAN OWNED IT. OWN?
WHO CAN OWN WHAT IS TIMELESS?
NOW THEY OWN, THEY FENCE, THEY
DIVIDE UP.
THEY SPOIL,
DESECRATE,
UTILIZE,
RUIN,
RAVAGE.

OUR PEOPLE ARE OUR PEOPLE NO MORE,
FOR THE LAND IS NO MORE.
IT DIED AND WE DIED.
THERE IS NO WAY BACK
AS LONG AS THE
PALENESS
IS OVER THE
LAND.

WILLIAM B. WILKERSON 1977

WHEN THE "I" CEASES
AND THE "WE"
BEGINS
THIS IS, THEN, THE POINT WHEN
WE ARE
FRIENDS.
NOT RACE   NOT COLOR
NOT SEX   NOT BELIEF
SHOULD CHANGE US EVER
FROM PEOPLE TO THINGS.

TAMARA H. BAREN

MULTIETHNIC BIBLIOGRAPHIES

AFRICA: AN ANNOTATED LIST OF PRINTED MATERIALS SUITABLE FOR CHILDREN.
U.S. COMMITTEE FOR UNICEF, 1968.

AMERICAN INDIANS: AN ANNOTATED BIBLIOGRAPHY OF RECOMMENDED RESOURCE
MATERIALS: ELEMENTARY GRADES. SAN JACINTO SCHOOL DISTRICT, 1971,
SAN JACINTO, CALIFORNIA.

"AND THE DARK-FACED CHILD, LISTENING": BOOKS ABOUT NEGROES FOR CHILDREN.
SCHOOL LIBRARIANS' ASSOCIATION OF MARIN COUNTY, 1969, SAN RAFAEL,
CALIFORNIA.

A BIBLIOGRAPHY OF NEGRO HISTORY AND CULTURE FOR YOUNG READERS. UNIVERSITY
OF PITTSBURGH PRESS, 1969.

THE BLACK AMERICANS: BOOKS FOR CHILDREN. OAKLAND PUBLIC SCHOOLS, 1970,
OAKLAND, CALIFORNIA.

THE BLACK EXPERIENCE IN CHILDREN'S BOOKS. BY AUGUSTA BAKER. NEW YORK
PUBLIC LIBRARY, 1971.

BOOKS FOR SPANISH-SPEAKING CHILDREN, SELECTED LISTS OF CHILDREN'S BOOKS AND
RECORDINGS. PREPARED BY THE ALA, 1966.

CHICANO: A SELECTED BIBLIOGRAPHY. INLAND LIBRARY SYSTEM, 1971, RIVERSIDE,
CALIFORNIA.

CHILDREN'S BOOKS ABOUT ASIAN ART. DOCENT COUNCIL, DEYOUNG MUSEUM,
SAN FRANCISCO, CALIFORNIA.

CHILDREN'S BOOKS ABOUT MEXICAN-AMERICANS AND CHILDREN IN MEXICO. COMPILED
BY NETTIE FRISHMAN. LOS ANGELES PUBLIC LIBRARY, 1968.

CHILDREN'S INTERRACIAL FICTION: AN UNSELECTIVE BIBLIOGRAPHY. AMERICAN
FEDERATION OF TEACHERS, 1969.

EDUCATOR'S GUIDE TO FREE SOCIAL STUDIES MATERIALS, 1977-78 ED. ROSELLA
LINSKIE, EDUCATIONAL CONSULTANT, EDUCATOR'S PROGRESS SERVICE, RANDOLPH,
WISCONSIN.

ENCYCLOPAEDIA OF ASSOCIATIONS. MARGARET FISK, ED., VOL. 1, NATIONAL
ORGANIZATIONS OF THE U.S. (10TH ED.) GALE RESEARCH, INCORPORATED.

ETHNIC INFORMATION SOURCES OF THE U.S. EDITED BY PAUL WASSERMAN AND JEAN
    MORGAN, GALE RESEARCH, INCORPORATED.

FOLOKLORE OF THE NORTH AMERICAN INDIANS: AN ANNOTATED BIBLIOGRAPHY. BY
    JUDITH C. ULLOM. GPO, 1969.

GETTING TO KNOW CHINA THROUGH BOOKS (KINDERGARTEN - 9TH GRADE). STANFORD
    AREA CHINESE CLUB, 1970, PALO ALTO, CALIFORNIA.

HISTORY AND CONTRIBUTIONS OF BLACK AMERICANS, SPANISH-SPEAKING AMERICANS
    LIVING TOGETHER IN THE U.S.A. IN THE WORLD. CHILDREN'S MUSIC CENTER,
    1969, LOS ANGELES, CALIFORNIA.

AN INDEX TO MULTI-ETHNIC TEACHING MATERIALS AND TEACHER RESOURCES.
    NATIONAL EDUCATION ASSOCIATION.

LATIN AMERICA: AN ANNOTATED LIST OF PRINTED MATERIALS SUITABLE FOR
    CHILDREN. U.S. COMMITTEE FOR UNICEF.

MINORITY CULTURES ANNOTATED BIBLIOGRAPHY: GRADES K - 12. MONTEREY COUNTY
    OFFICE OF EDUCATION, 1969, SALINAS, CALIFORNIA.

NATIVE AMERICANS: A SELECTIVE BIBLIOGRAPHY. ASSOCIATION OF CHILDREN'S
    LIBRARIANS OF NORTH CALIFORNIA, APRIL, 1972, DALY CITY, CALIFORNIA.

NEGROES IN CHILDREN'S BOOKS: A COMPREHENSIVE BIBLIOGRAPHY OF CHILDREN'S
    BOOKS ON AMERICAN NEGRO HISTORY AND CULTURE. JEFFERSON ELEMENTARY
    SCHOOL DISTRICT, APRIL, 1969, AND SUPPLEMENT/FEBRUARY, 1970, DALY CITY,
    CALIFORNIA.

SELECTED MEDIA ABOUT THE AMERICAN INDIAN FOR YOUNG CHILDREN, K - 3. BY
    SUZANNE C. CANE AND OTHERS. COMMONWEALTH OF MASSACHUSETTS, DEPARTMENT
    OF EDUCATION, 1971.

CROSS - CULTURAL REFERENCES

ALLPORT, GORDON W. THE NATURE OF PREJUDICE. DOUBLEDAY, 1958.

ANDERSON, DAVID D. AND ROBERT L. WRIGHT. DARK AND TANGLED PATH: RACE IN AMERICA. HOUGHTON, 1971.

BANKS, JAMES A., ED. TEACHING ETHNIC STUDIES: CONCEPTS AND STRATEGIES. NATIONAL COUNCIL FOR THE SOCIAL STUDIES, 1973.

BIRCH, HERBERT G. AND JOAN DYE GUSSOW. DISADVANTAGED CHILDREN: HEALTH, NUTRITION, AND SCHOOL FAILURE. HARCOURT, 1970.

CABRERA, ARTURO. "THE EDUCATIONAL NEEDS OF CHICANOS" PACIFICA TAPE LIBRARY.

CARLSON, LEWIS H. AND GEORGE A. COLBURN, EDS. IN THEIR PLACE: WHITE AMERICA DEFINES HER MINORITIES, 1850 - 1950. WILEY, 1972.

CHARNOFSKY, STANLEY. EDUCATING THE POWERLESS. WADSWORTH, 1971.

CLARK, KENNETH AND OTHERS. THE EDUCATIONALLY DEPRIVED: THE POTENTIAL FOR CHANGE. METROPOLITAN APPLIED RESEARCH CENTER.

COHEN, ROBERT. THE COLOR OF MAN. BANTAM, 1968.

COLES, ROBERT. CHILDREN OF CRISIS, VOL. I: A STUDY OF COURAGE AND FEAR. LITTLE, 1967.

-----, CHILDREN OF CRISIS, VOL. II: MIGRANTS, MOUNTAINEERS, AND SHARE-CROPPERS. LITTLE, 1972.

-----, CHILDREN OF CRISIS, VOL. III: THE SOUTH GOES NORTH. LITTLE, 1972.

DANIELS, ROGER AND HARRY L. KITANO. AMERICAN RACISM: EXPLORATION OF THE NATURE OF PREJUDICE. PRENTICE, 1969.

DAWSON, HELAINE S. ON THE OUTSKIRTS OF HOPE. MCGRAW, 1968.

EAGAN, JAMES M. LET'S TALK AND LISTEN. NATIONAL CONFERENCE OF CHRISTIANS AND JEWS, 1969.

EPSTEIN, CHARLOTTE. INTERGROUP RELATIONS FOR THE CLASSROOM TEACHER. HOUGHTON, 1968.

FORMAN, ROBERT E. BLACK GHETTOS, WHITE GHETTOS, AND SLUMS. PRENTICE, 1971.

FRANKLIN, JOHN HOPE AND OTHERS. ETHNICITY IN AMERICAN LIFE. ADL, 1971.

GINSBURG, HERBERT. THE MYTH OF THE DEPRIVED CHILD: POOR CHILDREN'S INTELLECT AND EDUCATION. PRENTICE, 1972.

GOODMAN, MARY ELLEN. A PRIMER FOR PARENTS: EDUCATING OUR CHILDREN FOR GOOD HUMAN RELATIONS. ADL, 1959.

-----. RACE AWARENESS IN YOUNG CHILDREN. (COLLIER) MACMILLAN, 1964.

GRAMBS, JEAN D. INTERGROUP EDUCATION: METHODS AND MATERIALS. PRENTICE, 1968.

-----. UNDERSTANDING INTERGROUP RELATIONS. NATIONAL EDUCATION ASSOCIATION, 1973.

GREEN, GERALD. BLOCKBUSTER. DOUBLEDAY, 1972.

GREEN, ROBERT L., ED. RACIAL CRISIS IN AMERICAN EDUCATION. FOLLETT, 1969.

GREGORY, DICK. NO MORE LIES: THE MYTH AND REALITY OF AMERICAN HISTORY. HARPER, 1970.

GREGORY, SUSAN. HEY, WHITE GIRL. NORTON, 1970.

HANDLIN, OSCAR. FIREBELL IN THE NIGHT: THE CRISIS IN CIVIL RIGHTS. LITTLE, !(¢$.

HEATON, MARGARET M. FEELINGS ARE FACTS. NATIONAL CONFERENCE OF CHRISTIANS AND JEWS, 1971.

HUGHES, LANGSTON. THE BOOK OF NEGRO FOLKLORE. DODD - MEAD, 1958.

HUTCHINS, ROBERT M. "THE SCHOOL MUST STAY," CENTER MAGAZINE, JAN/FEB 1973.

JACOBS, PAUL AND OTHERS. TO SERVE THE DEVIL, VOL. I: NATIVES AND SLAVES. RANDOM, 1971.

-----. TO SERVE THE DEVIL, VOL. II: COLONIALS AND SOJOURNERS. RANDOM, 1971.

JOHNSON, KENNETH R. TEACHING THE CULTURALLY DISADVANTAGED: A RATIONAL APPROACH. SRA, 1970.

JORDAN, JUNE. DRY VICTORIES. HOLT, 1972.

JOSEPH, STEPHEN, ED. THE ME NOBODY KNOWS: CHILDREN'S VOICES FROM THE GHETTO. AVON, 1969.

KANE, MICHAEL B. MINORITIES IN TEXTBOOKS: A STUDY OF THEIR TREATMENT IN
     SOCIAL STUDIES TEXTS. WATTS, 1970.

KNOWLES, LOUIS L. AND KENNETH PREWETT. INSTITUTIONAL RACISM IN AMERICA.
     PRENTICE, 1969.

KOHL, HERBERT R. THIRTY-SIX CHILDREN. NORTON, 1967.

KOZOL, JONATHAN. DEATH AT AN EARLY AGE. HOUGHTON, 1967.

-----. FREE SCHOOLS. HOUGHTON, 1972.

LAPIDES, FREDERICK R. AND DAVID BURROWS. RACISM: A CASEBOOK. CROWELL,
     1971.

LEVIN, HENRY M., ED. COMMUNITY CONTROL OF THE SCHOOLS. SIMON, 1970.

LOFTIS, ANNE. CALIFORNIA: WHERE THE TWAIN DID MEET. MACMILLAN, 1973.

MARDEN, CHARLES F. AND GLADYS MEYER. MINORITIES IN AMERICAN SOCIETY.
     VAN NOSTRAND, 1972.

MCWILLIAMS, CAREY. BROTHERS UNDER THE SKIN. REV. ED. LITTLE, 1964.

-----. FACTORIES IN THE FIELD: THE STORY OF THE MIGRATORY FARM LABORER IN
     CALIFORNIA. SHOE STRING, 1939.

MILLS, NICOLAUS, ED. THE GREAT SCHOOL BUS CONTROVERSY. TEACHER'S COLLEGE,
     COLUMBIA UNIVERSITY PRESS, 1973.

MIRTHES, CAROLINE AND THE CHILDREN OF P.S. 15. CAN'T YOU HEAR ME TALKING
     TO YOU? BANTAM, 1971.

MUI, Y.T. AND ROBERT GOODMAN AND ROBERT A. SPICER. THE MAGIC BRUSH.
     ISLAND HERITAGE BOOKS, 1974.

"NEW FACES OF PREJUDICE: WHAT TO DO." CALIFORNIA COUNCIL FOR THE SOCIAL
     STUDIES REVUE. SPRING, 1973.

NOAR, GERTRUDE. SENSITIZING TEACHERS TO ETHNIC GROUPS. ADL, 1973.

-----. THE TEACHER AND INTEGRATION. NATIONAL EDUCATION ASSOCIATION, 1966.

-----. TEACHING THE DISADVANTAGED. NATIONAL EDUCATION ASSOCIATION, 1972.

PETERS, WILLIAM. A CLASS DIVIDED. DOUBLEDAY, 1971.

PORTER, JUDITH D.R. BLACK CHILD, WHITE CHILD: THE DEVELOPMENT OF RACIAL ATTITUDES. HARVARD, 1971.

ROSE, PETER I. THEY AND WE: RACIAL AND ETHNIC RELATIONS IN THE UNITED STATES. RANDOM, 1964.

ROSENBERG, MAX. "TEST YOUR HRQ (HUMAN RELATIONS QUOTIENT)", TEACHER, MARCH, 1973.

ROSENTHAL, ROBERT AND LENORE JACOBSON. PYGMALION IN THE CLASSROOM: TEACHER EXPECTATION AND PUPILS' INTELLECTUAL DEVELOPMENT. HOLT, 1968.

RUSH, SHEILA AND CHRIS CLARK. HOW TO GET ALONG WITH BLACK PEOPLE: A HANDBOOK FOR WHITE FOLKS. THIRD PRESS, 1971.

RYAN, WILLIAM. BLAMING THE VICTIM. PANTHEON, 1971.

SCHWARTZ, BARRY N. AND ROBERT DISCH. WHITE RACISM: ITS HISTORY, PATHOLOGY, AND PRACTICE. DELL. 1970.

SILBERMAN, CHARLES E., COMP. THE OPEN CLASSROOM READER. RANDOM, 1973.

SMITH, ARTHUR L. TRANSRACIAL COMMUNICATION. PRENTICE, 1973.

STALVEY, LOIS MARK. THE EDUCATION OF A WASP. MORROW, 1970.

STEINBERG, STEPHEN. "THE LANGUAGE OF PREJUDICE," TODAY'S EDUCATION: JOURNAL OF THE NATIONAL EDUCATION ASSOCIATION. FEBRUARY, 1971.

STONE, JAMES C. AND DONALD P. DENEVI, ED. TEACHING MULTI CULTURAL POPULA-TIONS: FIVE HERITAGES. VAN NOSTRAND, 1971.

TAYLOR, RONALD B. SWEATSHOPS IN THE SUN: CHILD LABOR ON THE FARM. BEACON, 1973.

TAYLOR, WILLIAM L. HANGING TOGETHER: EQUALITY IN AN URBAN NATION. SIMON, 1971.

TUCKER, STERLING. WHY THE GHETTO MUST GO. PUBLIC AFFAIRS BUREAU, 1969.

WINECOFF, H.L. AND E. W. KELLEY, JR. TEACHERS, FREE OF PREJUDICE? (TAKE THIS TEST AND SEE.) INTEGRATED EDUCATION, 1969.

WOLFE, ANN E. DIFFERENCES CAN ENRICH OUR LIVES: HELPING CHILDREN PREPARE FOR CULTURAL DIVERSITY. PUBLIC AFFAIRS BUREAU, 1969.

YOUNG, MARGARET B. <u>HOW TO BRING UP YOUR CHILD WITHOUT PREJUDICE</u>. PUBLIC
    AFFAIRS BUREAU, 1965.

CHICANO AMERICAN REFERENCES

ACUNA, RUDOLFO. A MEXICAN AMERICAN CHRONICLE. AMERICAN BOOK, 1971.

-----. OCCUPIED AMERICA: THE CHICANO'S STRUGGLE TOWARD LIBERATION.
    CANFIELD, 1972.

BARRIO, RAYMOND. PLUM PLUM PICKERS: A NOVEL. CANFIELD, 1971.

BURMA, JOHN H., ED. MEXICAN AMERICANS IN THE UNITED STATES: A READER.
    CANFIELD, 1970.

COLES, ROBERT. THE OLD ONES OF MEXICO. UNIVERSITY OF NEW MEXICO, 1973.

DE LA GARZA, RUDOLPHE AND OTHERS. CHICANOS AND NATIVE AMERICANS: THE
    TERRITORIAL MINORITIES. PRENTICE, 1973.

"EDUCATION FOR THE SPANISH SPEAKING," THE NATIONAL ELEMENTARY PRINCIPAL.
    NOVEMBER, 1970.

FEHRENBACH, T.R. FIRE AND BLOOD: A HISTORY OF MEXICO. MACMILLAN, 1973.

FERNANDEZ, JUSTINO. A GUIDE TO MEXICAN ART: FROM ITS BEGINNINGS TO THE
    PRESENT. UNIVERSITY OF CHICAGO, 1969.

FLORES, JOSEPH A. SONGS AND DREAMS: MEXICAN AMERICAN LITERATURE.
    PENDULUM, 1972.

GALARZA, ERNESTO. BARRIO BOY. UNIVERSITY OF NOTRE DAME, 1971.

GONZALES, RODOLFO. I AM JOAQUIN/JO SOY JOAQUIN: AN EPIC POEM WITH A
    CHRONOLOGY OF PEOPLE AND EVENTS IN MEXICAN AND MEXICAN AMERICAN HISTORY.
    BANTAM, 1972.

GOMEZ, DAVID F. SOMOS CHICANOS: STRANGERS IN OUR LAND. BEACON, 1973.

HEINS, MARJORIE. STRICTLY GHETTO PROPERTY: THE STORY OF LOS SIETE DE LE
    RAZA. RAMPARTS, 1972

IDUARTE, ANDRES. NINO: CHILD OF THE MEXICAN REVOLUTION. PRAEGER, 1971.

JOHNSON, HENRY SIOUX AND JAMES HERNANDEZ. EDUCATING THE MEXICAN AMERICAN.
    JUDSON, 1971.

JONES, EDWARD H. AND MARGARET S. JONES. ARTS AND CRAFTS OF THE MEXICAN
    PEOPLE. RITCHIE, 1971.

LITSINGER, DELORES ESCOBAR. THE CHALLENGE OF TEACHING MEXICAN AMERICAN
    STUDENTS. AMERICAN BOOK, 1973.

MCWILLIAMS, CAREY. NORTH FROM MEXICO: THE SPANISH-SPEAKING PEOPLE OF THE
    UNITED STATES. GREENWOOD, 1949.

MEIER, MATTHEW S. AND FELICIANO RIVERA. THE CHICANOS: A HISTORY OF THE
    MEXICAN AMERICAN. HILL, 1972.

MORIN, RAUL. AMONG THE VALIENT. BORDEN, 1963.

NAVA, JULIAN. MEXICAN AMERICANS: A BRIEF LOOK AT THEIR HISTORY. ADL,
    1970.

ORTEGO, PHILIP D., ED. WE ARE CHICANOS: AN ANTHOLOGY OF MEXICAN AMERICAN
    LITERATURE. WASHINGTON SQUARE, 1973.

PAREDES, AMERICO. "WITH HIS PISTOL IN HIS HAND": A BORDER BALLAD AND ITS
    HERO. UNIVERSITY OF TEXAS, 1958.

-----, ED. FOLKTALES OF MEXICO. UNIVERSITY OF CHICAGO, 1970.

QUINN, ANTHONY. THE ORIGINAL SIN: A SELF-PORTRAIT. LITTLE, 1972.

QUIRARTE, JACINTO. MEXICAN AMERICAN ARTISTS. UNIVERSITY OF TEXAS, 1973.

RENDON, ARMANDO B. CHICANO MANIFESTO. MACMILLAN, 1971.

ROBE, STANLEY L. MEXICAN TALES AND LEGENDS FROM VERACRUZ. UNIVERSITY OF
    CALIFORNIA, 1971.

ROBINSON, CECIL. WITH THE EARS OF STRANGERS: THE MEXICAN IN AMERICAN
    LITERATURE. UNIVERSITY OF ARIZONA, 1963.

ROUVEROL, JEAN. PANCHO VILLA: A BIOGRAPHY. DOUBLEDAY, 1972.

SAMORA, JULIAN. LOS MOJOADOS: THE WETBACK STORY. UNIVERSITY OF NOTRE
    DAME, 1971.

SHEARER, TONY. LORD OF THE DAWN: QUETZACOATL. NATUREGRAPH, 1971.

SHOCKLEY, JOHN STAPLES. CHICANO REVOLT IN A TEXAS TOWN. UNIVERSITY OF
    NOTRE DAME, 1973.

SIMMEN, EDWARD, ED. PAIN AND PROMISE: THE CHICANO TODAY. NAL, 1972.

----, ED. THE CHICANO: FROM CARICATURE TO SELF PORTRAIT. NAL, 1972.

SIMPSON, LESLEY BYRD. MANY MEXICOS. UNIVERSITY OF CALIFORNIA, 1967.

SMITH, BRADLEY. MEXICO: A HISTORY IN ART. DOUBLEDAY, 1971.

STEINBECK, JOHN. THE PEARL. VIKING, 1947.

STEINER, STAN. LA RAZA: THE MEXICAN AMERICANS. HARPER, 1970.

STEVENSON, ROBERT. MUSIC IN MEXICO: A HISTORICAL SURVEY. APOLLO, 1952.

TEBBEL, JOHN AND RAMON RUIZ. SOUTH BY SOUTHWEST: THE MEXICAN AMERICAN AND
     HIS HERITAGE. DOUBLEDAY, 1969.

TOOR, FRANCES. TREASURY OF MEXICAN FOLKWAYS: THE CUSTOMS, MYTHS, FOLKLORE,
     TRADITIONS, BELIEFS, FIESTAS, AND SONGS OF THE MEXICAN PEOPLE. CROWN,
     1967.

BLACK AMERICAN REFERENCES

ACHEBE, CHINUA. THINGS FALL APART. ASTOR-HONOR, 1959.

ADAMS, RUSSELL L. GREAT NEGROES, PAST AND PRESENT. AFRO-AM., 1969.

ADOFF, ARNOLD, ED. THE POETRY OF BLACK AMERICA: ANTHOLOGY OF THE 20TH
    CENTURY. HARPER, 1973.

ANGELOU, MAYA. I KNOW WHY THE CAGED BIRD SINGS. RANDOM, 1970.

BALDWIN, JAMES. NO NAME IN THE STREET. DIAL, 1972.

BAMBARA, TONI CADE. GORILLA, MY LOVE. RANDOM, 1972.

BANKS, JAMES A. TEACHING THE BLACK EXPERIENCE: METHODS AND MATERIALS.
    FEARON, 1970.

----- AND JEAN GRAMBS, EDS. BLACK SELF CONCEPT: IMPLICATIONS FOR
    EDUCATION AND SOCIAL SCIENCE. MCGRAW, 1972.

BARRETT, LEONARD E. SOUL-FORCE: AFRICAN HERITAGE IN AFRO-AMERICAN RELIGION.
    DOUBLEDAY, 1974.

BENNETT, LERONE. BEFORE THE MAYFLOWER: A HISTORY OF THE NEGRO IN AMERICA,
    1619 - 1966. JOHNSON, 1966.

-----. WHAT MANNER OF MAN: A BIOGRAPHY OF MARTIN LUTHAR KING, JR. JOHNSON,
    1964.

BERRY, FAITH, ED. GOOD MORNING REVOLUTION: THE UNCOLLECTED SOCIAL PROTEST
    WRITINGS BY LANGSTON HUGHES. LAWRENCE HILL, 1973.

"BLACK MUSIC," THE BLACK SCHOLAR, SUMMER, 1972.

BROWN, CLAUDE. MANCHILD IN THE PROMISED LAND. MACMILLAN, 1965.

CADE, TONI, ED. THE BLACK WOMAN: AN ANTHOLOGY. SIGNET, 1970.

CHASE, JUDITH WRAGG. AFRO-AMERICAN ART AND CRAFT. VAN NOSTRAND, 1971.

CHISHOLM, SHIRLEY. UNBOUGHT AND UNBOSSED. HOUGHTON, 1970.

DILLARD. J.L. BLACK ENGLISH. RANDOM, 1972.

ELLISON, RALPH. INVISIBLE MAN. RANDOM, 1952.

FADER, DANIEL. THE NAKED CHILDREN. MACMILLAN, 1971.

FELDMAN, SUSAN, ED. AFRICAN MYTHS AND TALES. DELL, 1970.

FRANKLIN, JOHN HOPE. FROM SLAVERY TO FREEDOM: A HISTORY OF THE AMERICAN
     NEGROES. KNOPF, 1967.

----- AND THE EDITORS OF TIME-LIFE BOOKS. AN ILLUSTRATED HISTORY OF BLACK
     AMERICANS. TIME-LIFE, 1970.

GAINES, ERNEST J. THE AUTOBIOGRAPHY OF MISS JANE PITTMAN. DIAL, 1971.

GARDI, NENE. AFRICAN CRAFTS AND CRAFTSMEN. VON NOSTRAND, 1970.

GRAMBS, JEAN D. AND JOHN C. CARR. BLACK IMAGE: EDUCATION COPES WITH
     COLOR. BROWN, 1971.

GRIER, WILLIAM H. AND PRICE M. COBBS. BLACK RAGE. BASIC, 1968.

GUY, ROSA, ED. CHILDREN OF LONGING. HOLT, 1970.

HAMILTON, CHARLES V. THE BLACK PREACHER IN AMERICA. MORROW, 1972.

HARRIS, MIDDLETON AND OTHERS. THE BLACK BOOK. RANDOM, 1974.

HARRISON-ROSS, PHYLLIS, M.D. AND BARBARA WYDEN. THE BLACK CHILD - A
     PARENT'S GUIDE: HOW TO OVERCOME PROBLEMS OF RAISING BLACK CHILDREN IN
     A WHITE WORLD. WYDEN, 1973.

HIMES, CHESTER. BLACK ON BLACK: BABY SISTER AND SELECTED WRITINGS.
     DOUBLEDAY, 1973.

HUGHES, LANGSTON, ED. THE BOOK OF NEGRO HUMOR. DODD, 1966.

----- AND ARNA BONTEMPS, EDS. THE BOOK OF NEGRO FOLKLORE. DODD, 1958.

-----, MILTON MELTZER, AND C. ERIC LINCOLN. A PICTORIAL HISTORY OF BLACK
     AMERICANS. CROWN, 1973.

JONES, REGINALD L., ED. BLACK PSYCHOLOGY. HARPER, 1972.

JORDAN, WINTHROP D. WHITE OVER BLACK: AMERICAN ATTITUDES TOWARD THE NEGRO.
     UNIVERSITY OF NORTH CAROLINA PRESS, 1968.

JOSEY, E.J., ED. WHAT BLACK LIBRARIANS ARE SAYING. SCARECROW, 1972.

KATZ, WILLIAM LOREN. THE BLACK WEST. DOUBLEDAY, 1973.

KILLENS, JOHN O. AND THEN WE HEARD THE THUNDER. KNOPF, 1963.

LACY, DAN.   THE WHITE USE OF BLACKS IN AMERICA.   ATHENEUM, 1972.

LAUDE, JEAN.   THE ARTS OF BLACK AFRICA.   UNIVERSITY OF CALIFORNIA, 1971.

LERNA, GERDA.   BLACK WOMAN IN WHITE AMERICA.   PANTHEON, 1972.

LOMAX, ALAN AND ABDUL RAOUL, EDS.   3,000 YEARS OF BLACK POETRY: AN ANTHOLOGY.
     DODD, 1970.

MAJOR, CLARENCE, ED.   THE NEW BLACK POETRY.   INTERNATIONAL 1969.

MALCOM X AND ALEX HALEY.   THE AUTOBIOGRAPHY OF MALCOM X.   GROVE, 1965.

MCKAY, CLAUDE.   A LONG WAY FROM HOME.   ARNO, 1937.

MERIWETHER, LOUISE.   DADDY WAS A NUMBERS RUNNER.   PRENTICE, 1970.

MOODY, ANNE.   COMING OF AGE IN MISSISSIPPI.   DIAL, 1968.

MORRISON, TONI.   THE BLUEST EYE.   HOLT, 1970.

NELSON, HART M. AND OTHERS, EDS.   THE BLACK CHURCH IN AMERICA.   BASIC, 1971.

PINKNEY, ALPHONSO.   BLACK AMERICANS.   PRENTICE, 1969.

RICHARDS, EUGENE.   FEW COMFORTS OR SURPRISES: THE ARKANSAS DELTA.   MIT,
     1973.
SILBERMAN, CHARLES E.   CRISIS IN BLACK AND WHITE.   RANDOM, 1964.

SIRKIS, NANCY.   ONE FAMILY.   LITTLE, 1970.

STAPLES, ROBERT, ED.   THE BLACK FAMILY.   WADSWORTH, 1970.

SOUTHERN, EILEEN.   THE MUSIC OF BLACK AMERICANS: A HISTORY.   NORTON, 1971.

SOWELL, THOMAS.   BLACK EDUCATION: MYTHS AND TRAGEDIES.   MCKAY, 1972.

TOOMER, JEAN.   CANE.   LIVERIGHT, C 1923.

WALKER, ALICE.   IN LOVE AND TROUBLE: STORIES OF BLACK WOMEN.   HARCOURT,
     1973.

WALLS, DWAYNE E.   THE CHICKENBONE SPECIAL.   HARCOURT, 1971.

WALTON, ORTIZ M.   MUSIC: BLACK, WHITE, AND BLUE: A SOCIOLOGICAL SURVEY OF
     THE USE AND MISUSE OF AFRO-AMERICAN MUSIC.   MORROW, 1972.

WASHINGTON, JOSEPH R., JR. BLACK RELIGION: THE NEGRO AND CHRISTIANITY IN THE UNITED STATES. BEACON, 1964.

-----. MARRIAGE IN BLACK AND WHITE. BEACON, 1970.

WILHELM, SIDNEY. WHO NEEDS THE NEGRO? SCHENKMAN, 1970.

WILLIAMS, JOHN A. THE MAN WHO CRIED "I AM!" LITTLE, 1967.

WRIGHT, NATHAN. WHAT BLACK EDUCATORS ARE SAYING. HAWTHORN, 1970.

WRIGHT, RICHARD. NATIVE SON. HARPER, 1940.

WRIGHT, SARA E. THIS CHILD'S GONNA LIVE. DELACORTE, 1969.

YETTE, SAMUEL F. THE CHOICE: THE ISSUE OF BLACK SURVIVAL IN AMERICA. PUTNAM, 1971.

YOUNG, CARLENE. BLACK EXPERIENCE: ANALYSIS AND SYNTHESIS. LESWING, 1972.

ASIAN AMERICAN REFERENCES

ABE, YUJI, ED. <u>MODERN JAPANESE PRINTS: A CONTEMPORARY SELECTION</u>. TUTTLE, 1970.

AGONCILLO, TEODORO A. <u>A SHORT STORY OF THE PHILIPPINES</u>. NAL, 1969.

----- AND MILIGROS C. GUERRERO. <u>HISTORY OF THE FILIPINO PEOPLE</u>. QUEZON CITY, PHILIPPINES: MALAYA, 1970.

AQUINO, GUADENCIO AND OTHERS. <u>PHILIPPINE FOLKTALES</u>. QUEZON CITY, PHILIPPINES: ALEMAR-PHOENIC, 1969.

BAILEY, PAUL. <u>CONCENTRATION CAMP, U.S.A.</u> TOWER, 1972.

BANG, IM AND YI RYUK. <u>KOREAN FOLK TALES: IMPS, GHOSTS, AND FAIRIES</u>. TUTTLE, 1963.

BARNSTONE, WILLIS. <u>NEW FACES OF CHINA</u>. INDIANA UNIVERSITY PRESS, 1973.

BARTH, GUNTHER. <u>BITTER STRENGTH: A HISTORY OF THE CHINESE IN THE UNITED STATES, 1850 - 1870</u>. HARVARD UNIVERSITY PRESS, 1964.

BUCK, PEARL S. <u>THE GOOD EARTH</u>. DAY, 1965.

CHANG, ISABELLE C. <u>CHINESE FAIRY TALES</u>. SCHOCKEN, 1965.

CHEN, JACK. <u>A YEAR IN UPPER FELICITY: LIFE IN A CHINESE VILLAGE DURING THE CULTURAL REVOLUTION</u>. MACMILLAN, 1973.

CHENG-TSU, WU, ED. <u>CHINK: EVIDENCE OF THE ANTI-CHINESE PREJUDICE PERVADING OUR COUNTRY</u>. WORLD, 1972.

CHEON, KANG-SIE. <u>A BUTTERFLY'S DREAM AND OTHER CHINESE TALES</u>. TUTTLE, 1971.

CHIN, FRANK. "CONFESSIONS OF NUMBER ONE SON," <u>RAMPARTS</u>, FEBRUARY, 1973.

<u>CHINESE AMERICANS: SCHOOL AND COMMUNITY PROBLEMS</u>. INTEGRATED EDUCATION, 1972.

CHU, DANIEL AND SAMUEL CHU. <u>PASSAGE TO THE GOLDEN GATE: A HISTORY OF THE CHINESE IN AMERICA TO 1910</u>. DOUBLEDAY, 1967.

COLOMBO, FURIO. <u>THE CHINESE</u>. GROSSMAN, 1972.

CONROY, HILLARY AND T. SCOTT MIYAKAWA, EDS. <u>ACROSS THE PACIFIC: HISTORICAL AND SOCIOLOGICAL STUDIES OF JAPANESE IMMIGRATION AND ASSIMILATION</u>. ABC-CLIO, 1972.

COOLIDGE, MARY R. CHINESE IMMIGRATION. ARNO, 1969.

DANIELS, ROGER. CONCENTRATION CAMPS, U.S.A. / JAPANESE AMERICANS AND WORLD
     WAR II. HOLT, 1972.

-----. POLITICS OF PREJUDICE: THE ANTI-JAPANESE MOVEMENT IN CALIFORNIA
     AND THE STRUGGLE FOR JAPANESE EXCLUSION. PETER SMITH, 1962.

DAZAI, OSAMU. NO LONGER HUMAN. NEW DIRECTIONS, 1973.

DIETZ, BETTY WARNER AND THOMAS CHOONBAI PARKS, EDS. FOLK SONGS OF CHINA,
     JAPAN, AND KOREA. DAY, 1964.

EMBREY, SUE KUNITOMI, ED. THE LOST YEARS: 1942 - 1946. MOONLIGHT PUBLI-
     CATIONS, 1972.

HENDERSON, HAROLD G. HAIKU IN ENGLISH. TUTTLE, 1967.

HOSOKAWA, BILL. NISEI: THE QUIET AMERICANS. MORROW, 1969.

HOUSTON, JEANNE WAKATSUKI AND JAMES D. HOUSTON. FAREWELL TO MANZANAR.
     HOUGHTON, 1973.

HSU, FRANCIS. AMERICANS AND CHINESE: PURPOSE AND FULFILLMENT IN GREAT
     CIVILIZATIONS. NATURAL HISTORY, 1972.

-----. CHALLENGE TO THE AMERICAN DREAM: THE CHINESE IN THE UNITED STATES.
     WADSWORTH, 1971.

HSUEH-CHIN, TSAO. DREAMS OF THE RED CHAMBER. TWAYNE, 1958.

INADA, LAWSON FUSAO. BEFORE THE WAR: POEMS AS THEY HAPPENED. MORROW, 1971/

ISHIGO, ESTELLE. LONE HEART MOUNTAIN. ANDERSON, 1972.

KIM, WARREN Y. KOREANS IN AMERICA. PO CHIN CHAI PRINTING COMPANY, 1971.

KITANO, HARRY. JAPANESE AMERICANS: THE EVOLUTION OF A SUB-CULTURE.
     PRENTICE, 1969.

LYMAN, STANFORD. THE ASIAN IN THE WEST. DESERT RESEARCH INSTITUTE,
     UNIVERSITY OF NEVADA PRESS, 1970.

MATSUBARA, HISAKO. THE TALE OF THE SHINING PRINCESS. KODANSHA, 1966.

MCCUNE, EVELYN. THE ARTS OF KOREA: AN ILLUSTRATED HISTORY. TUTTLE, 1970.

MCCUNE, SHANNON. KOREA'S HERITAGE. TUTTLE, 1964.

MCWILLIAMS, CAREY. PREJUDICE: JAPANESE AMERICANS: SYMBOL OF RACIAL INTOLERANCE. SHOE STRING, 1971.

MILLER, STUART CREIGHTON. THE UNWELCOME IMMIGRANT: THE AMERICAN IMAGE OF THE CHINESE 1785 - 1882. UNIVERSITY OF CALIFORNIA PRESS, 1969.

MISHIMA, YUKIO. THE TEMPLE OF DAWN. KNOPF, 1973.

MITFORD, A.B. (LORD REDESDALE). TALES OF OLD JAPAN. TUTTLE, 1966.

MIYAMOTO, KAZUO. HAWAII - END OF THE RAINBOW. TUTTLE, 1964.

MUNSTERBERG, HUGO. ART OF THE FAR EAST. ABRAMS, 1968.

MYER, DILLON S. UPROOTED AMERICANS: THE JAPANESE AMERICANS AND THE WAR RELOCATION AUTHORITY. UNIVERSITY OF ARIZONA PRESS, 1971.

NAKANE, CHIE. JAPANESE SOCIETY. UNIVERSITY OF CALIFORNIA PRESS, 1970.

OGAWA, DENNIS, ED. FROM JAPS TO JAPANESE. MCCUTCHAN, 1971.

OKADA, JOHN. NO-NO BOY. TUTTLE, 1973.

OKIMOTO, DANIEL. AMERICAN IN DISGUISE. WALKER/WEATHERHILL, 1971.

QUANG, ROSE. CHINESE WRITTEN CHARACTERS: THEIR WIT AND WISDOM. BEACON, 1973.

REXROTH, KENNETH. ONE HUNDRED POEMS FROM THE CHINESE. NEW DIRECTIONS, 1956.

-----. ONE HUNDRED POEMS FROM THE JAPANESE. NEW DIRECTIONS, 1955.

SANSOM, G.B. JAPAN: A SHORT CULTURAL STUDY. APPLETON, 1962.

SUNG, BETTY LEE. MOUNTAIN OF GOLD: THE STORY OF THE CHINESE IN AMERICA. MACMILLAN, 1967.

-----. THE STORY OF THE CHINESE IN AMERICA. MACMILLAN, 1971.

TACHIKI, AMY AND OTHERS, EDS. ROOTS: AN ASIAN AMERICAN READER. U.C.L.A. ASIAN AMERICAN STUDIES CENTER, 1971.

TAKASHIMA, S. A CHILD IN PRISON CAMP. TUNDRA, 1971.

UCHIDA, YOSHIKO. JOURNEY TO TOPAZ. SCRIBNER, 1971.

WONG, JADE. <u>FIFTH CHINESE DAUGHTER</u>. HARPER, 1950.

YOSHIDA, JIM AND BILL HOSAKAWA. <u>THE TWO WORLDS OF JIM YOSHIDA</u>. MORROW, 1972.

NATIVE AMERICAN REFERENCES

ADAIR, JOHN AND KURT W. DEUSCHLE. THE PEOPLE'S HEALTH: MEDICINE AND ANTHROPOLOGY IN A NAVAJO COMMUNITY. APLLETON, 1970.

AIELLO, CONSTANTINE, ED. OO-OONAH ART. TAOS PUEBLO GOVERNOR'S OFFICE, 1970.

ALCATRAZ IS NOT AN ISLAND, BY INDIANS OF ALL TRIBES. WINGBOW, 1972.

ALLEN, TERRY, ED. THE WHISPERING WIND: POETRY BY YOUNG AMERICAN INDIANS. DOUBLEDAY, 1972.

AMERICAN INDIAN ART: FORM AND TRADITION. DUTTON, 1972.

"THE AMERICAN INDIAN," ART IN AMERICA. JULY-AUGUST, 1972.

ANDRIST, RALPH K. THE LONG DEATH: THE LAST DAYS OF THE PLAINS INDIANS. MACMILLAN, 1969.

ASTROV, MARGOT. AMERICAN INDIAN PROSE AND POETRY. DAY, 1946.

BAHTI, TOM. AN INTRODUCTION TO SOUTHWESTERN INDIAN ARTS AND CRAFTS. KC PUBLISHERS, 1966.

BARRETT, S.M., ED. GERONIMO, HIS OWN STORY. BALLENTINE, 1971.

BERGER, THOMAS. LITTLE BIG MAN. DIAL, 1964.

BIERHORST, JOHN, ED. IN THE TRAIL OF THE WIND: AMERICAN INDIAN POEMS AND RITUAL ORATIONS. FARRAR, 1971.

BIRD, TRAVELER. TELL THEM THEY LIE: THE SEQUOIA MYTH. WESTERNLORE, 1971.

BIRKET-SMITH, KAJ. ESKIMOS. CROWN, 1971.

BARLAND, HAL. WHEN THE LEGENDS DIE. LIPPINCOTT, 1963.

BRANDON, WILLIAM, ED. THE AMERICAN HERITAGE BOOK OF INDIANS. DELL, 1961.

-----, ED. MAGIC WORLD: AMERICAN INDIAN SONGS AND POEMS. MORROW, 1971.

BROWN, DEE. BURY MY HEART AT WOUNDED KNEE: AN INDIAN HISTORY OF THE AMERICAN WEST. HOLT, 1970.

BURNETTE, ROBERT. THE TORTURED AMERICANS. PRENTICE, 1971.

CAHN, EDGAR S., ED. OUR BROTHER'S KEEPER: THE INDIAN IN WHITE AMERICA. WORLD, 1969.

COLLIER, PETER. WHEN SHALL THEY REST? THE CHEROKEES' LONG STRUGGLE WITH AMERICA. HOLT, 1973.

CORNPLANTER, JESSE J. LEGENDS OF THE LONGHOUSE. KENNIKAT, 1938.

CURTIS, EDWARD S. IN A SACRED MANNER WE LIVE: PHOTOGRAPHY OF THE NORTH AMERICAN INDIAN. BARRE, 1973.

CURTIS, NATALIE, ED. THE INDIAN'S BOOK: SONGS AND LEGENDS OF THE AMERICAN INDIANS. PETER SMITH, 1950.

DELORIA, VINE, JR. CUSTER DIED FOR YOUR SINS: AN INDIAN MANIFESTO. MACMILLAN, 1969.

DEMENIL, ADELAIDE AND WILLIAM REID. OUT OF THE SILENCE. HARPER, 1972.

DENSMORE, FRANCES. STUDY OF INDIAN MUSIC. SHOREY, 1941.

DOCKSTADER, FREDERICK. INDIAN ART IN NORTH AMERICA: ARTS AND CRAFTS. NEW YORK GRAPHIC, 1968.

EMBREE, EDWIN R. INDIANS OF THE AMERICAS. HOUGHTON, 1939.

FEDER, NORMAN. TWO HUNDRED YEARS OF NORTH AMERICAN INDIAN ART. PRAEGER, 1972.

FELDMAN, SUSAN, ED. THE STORYTELLING STONE: MYTHS AND TALES OF THE AMERICAN INDIANS. DELL, 1965.

FIRE, JOHN/LAME DEER AND RICHARD ERDOES. LAME DEER: SEEKER OF VISIONS. SIMON, 1972.

FORBES, JACK D., ED. THE INDIAN IN AMERICA'S PAST. PRENTICE, 1964.

-----. NATIVE AMERICANS OF CALIFORNIA AND NEVADA. NATUREGRAPH, 1969.

FRIER, RALPH AND NATASHA. THE ONLY GOOD INDIAN: THE HOLLYWOOD GOSPEL. DRAMA BOOK SHOP, 1973.

FUCHS, ESTELLE AND ROBERT J. HAVIGHURST. TO LIVE ON THIS EARTH: AMERICAN INDIAN EDUCATION. DOUBLEDAY, 1972.

GRIDLEY, MARION E. AMERICAN INDIAN WOMEN. HAWTHORN, 1974.

HEIZER, R.F. AND M.A. WHIPPLE, EDS. THE CALIFORNIA INDIANS: A SOURCE BOOK. UNIVERSITY OF CALIFORNIA PRESS, 1971.

HILLERMAN, TONY. THE BLESSING WAY. HARPER, 1970.

-----. DANCE HALL OF THE DEAD. HARPER, 1973.

JACOBS, WILBUR. DISPOSSESSING THE AMERICAN INDIAN. SCRIBNER, 1972.

JONES, CHARLES, ED. LOOK AT THE MOUNTAIN TOP. GOUSHA, 1972.

JOSEPHY, ALVIN M., JR. THE INDIAN HERITAGE OF AMERICA. KNOPF, 1968.

-----. RED POWER: THE AMERICAN INDIANS' FIGHT FOR FREEDOM. MCGRAW, 1971.

KROEBER, THEODORA. ISHI IN TWO WORLDS: A BIOGRAPHY OF THE LAST WILD
     INDIAN IN NORTHERN AMERICA. UNIVERSITY OF CALIFORNIA PRESS, 1971.

LA FARGE, OLIVER. A PICTORIAL HISTORY OF THE AMERICAN INDIAN. CROWN, 1956.

LA POINTE, FRANK. THE SIOUX TODAY. MACMILLAN, 1972.

LEGENDS TOLD BY THE OLD PEOPLE. ADOLPH HUNGRY WOLF, 1972.

LEWIS, RICHARD, ED. I BREATHE A NEW SONG: POEMS OF THE ESKIMO. SIMON, 1972.

MARKOOSIE. HARPOON OF THE HUNTER. MCGILL/QUEEN'S UNIVERSITY PRESS, 1970.

MARRIOTT, ALICE. MARIA: THE POTTER OF SAN ILDEFONSO. UNIVERSITY OF
     OKLAHOMA PRESS, 1948.

MASSON, MARCELLE. A BAG OF BONES: LEGENDS OF THE WINTU INDIANS OF
     NORTHERN CALIFORNIA. NATUREGRAPH, 1966.

MCLUHAN, T.C., ED. TOUCH THE EARTH: A SELF PORTRAIT OF THE INDIAN EXISTENCE.
     SWALLOW, 1973.

MEYER, WILLIAM. NATIVE AMERICANS: THE NEW INDIAN RESISTANCE. INTERNATIONAL,
     1971.

MITCHELL, EMERSON B. AND T.D. ALLEN. MIRACLE HILL: THE STORY OF A NAVAJO
     BOY. UNIVERSITY OF OKLAHOMA PRESS, 1967.

MOMADAY, N. SCOTT. THE WAY TO RAINY MOUNTAIN. UNIVERSITY OF NEW MEXICO
     PRESS, 1969.

-----. HOUSE MADE OF DAWN. HARPER, 1968.

NEIHARDT, JOHN G. WHEN THE TREE FLOWERED: AN AUTHENTIC TALE OF THE OLD
     SIOUX WORLD. UNIVERSITY OF NEBRASKA PRESS, 1970.

PARKER, CHIEF EVERETT AND OLEDOSKA. THE SECRET OF NO FACE (AN IREOKWA EPIC.) NATUREGRAPH, 1972.

PELLETIER, WILFRED AND TED POOLE. NO FOREIGN LAND: THE BIOGRAPHY OF A NORTH AMERICAN INDIAN. PANTHEON, 1973.

PRATSON, FREDERICK J. LAND OF THE FOUR DIRECTIONS: A PORTRAIT OF AMERICAN INDIAN LIFE TODAY. CHATHAM, 1970.

ROTHENBERG, JEROME, ED. SHAKING THE PUMPKIN: TRADITIONAL POETRY OF THE INDIAN NORTH AMERICAS. DOUBLEDAY, 1972.

SANCHEZ, THOMAS. RABBIT ROSS. KNOPF, 1973.

SANDOZ, MARI. THE BATTLE OF THE LITTLE BIG HORN. LIPPINCOTT, 1966.

-----. HORSECATCHER. WESTMINSTER, 1957.

SCHUSKY, E. THE RIGHT TO BE INDIAN. INDIAN HISTORIAN, 1970.

SENUNGETUK, JOSEPH. GIVE OR TAKE A CENTURY: AN ESKIMO CHRONICLE. INDIAN HISTORIAN, 1970.

STORM, HYEMEYOHSTS. SEVEN ARROWS. HARPER, 1972.

STUMP, SARAIN. THERE IS MY PEOPLE SLEEPING: THE ETHNIC POEM DRAWINGS OF SARAIN STUMP. GRAY'S, 1970.

TEXTBOOKS AND THE AMERICAN INDIAN. INDIAN HISTORIAN, 1970.

VAN EVERY, DALE. THE DAY THE SUN DIED. LITTLE, 1971.

VOGEL, VIRGIL J. THIS COUNTRY WAS OURS: A DOCUMENTARY HISTORY OF THE AMERICAN INDIAN. HARPER, 1972.

-----. THE INDIAN IN AMERICAN HISTORY. INTEGRATED EDUCATION, 1968.

WATERS, FRANK. THE MAN WHO KILLED THE DEER. SWALLOW, 1942.

-----. BOOK OF THE HOPI. VIKING, 1963.

-----. PUMPKIN SEED POINT: BEING WITHIN THE HOPI. SWALLOW, 1969.

WISE, JENNINGS CROPPER. THE RED MAN IN THE NEW WORLD DRAMA. MACMILLAN, 1971.

WITT, SHIRLEY HILL AND STAN STEINER, EDS. <u>THE WAY: AN ANTHOLOGY OF AMERICAN INDIAN LITERATURE</u>. KNOPF, 1972.

<u>THE ZUNIS: SELF PORTRAYAL</u>. UNIVERSITY OF NEW MEXICO PRESS, 1972.

MULTIETHNIC FILMS AND FILMSTRIPS (KEY: P=PRIMARY I=INTERMEDIATE A=ADVANCED)

THE CANADIANS (I-A) THE FIVE FILMSTRIPS PRESENT THE HERITAGE OF THE CANADIANS, SIMILAR TO THAT OF THE UNITED STATES IN HISTORICAL DEVELOPMENT, WITH THE INFLUENCE OF THE NATIVE INDIANS, EARLY SETTLERS OF FRENCH AND ENGLISH BACKGROUND, AND THE IMMIGRANTS OF MANY CULTURES OF THE WORLD.

CHILDREN AROUND THE WORLD (P-I) THE FORTY-EIGHT PICTURE STORY STUDY PRINTS OF THIS SET INCLUDE REPRESENTATIVE CHILDREN AND INFORMATION OF MANY OF THE COUNTRIES AND CULTURES OF THE WORLD.

COLORS OF MAN (P-I) A MULTI-MEDIA ACTIVITY KIT TO INTRODUCE CHILDREN TO THE UNDERSTANDING OF SKIN COLOR, DIFFERENCES AND SIMILARITIES AMONG ALL PEOPLE.

THE EYE OF THE STORM (I-A) A THIRD GRADE TEACHER INSTRUCTS HER CLASS TOWARD THE DEVELOPMENT OF THE CONCEPT OF PREJUDICE BY DIVIDING THE CLASS AND SUBJECTING EACH HALF, IN TURN, TO DISCRIMINATION BASED ON FALSE PREMISES.

FABLES AND FACTS (P-I-A) THE EIGHT FILMSTRIPS INCLUDE TRADITIONAL STORIES FROM CULTURES OF THE GREEK, AUSTRALIAN, FAR EAST, AMERICAN INDIAN, AND OTHERS. THE FILMSTRIPS DO A CREDITABLE JOB CONTRASTING THE BELIEFS OF FABLES AND THE TRUTH OF FACT.

FOLK AND FAIRY TALES (P-I-A) THE EIGHT CASSETTES PROVIDE LISTENING EXPERIENCES OF FOLK AND FAIRY TALES FROM MANY CULTURES AROUND THE WORLD, AND DOES AN EXCELLENT JOB PROVIDING A STIMULATION FOR AWARENESS AMONG CHILDREN OF THE UNIVERSAL ELEMENTS AMONG THE CULTURES OF THE WORLD.

FOLK STORIES FROM OTHER LANDS (P-I-A) SIX FILMSTRIPS INCLUDE FOLK STORIES FROM SWEDEN, ENGLAND, TURKEY, CENTRAL EUROPE, AND CHINA.

FOLKTALES (P-I-A) FOUR FILMSTRIPS EACH DEPICTING A FOLKTALE OF A DIFFERENT ETHNIC CULTURE: UKRANIAN, JAPANESE, SCOTTISH, AND TURKISH.

FOLK TALES FROM MANY LANDS (P-I-A) SIX FILMSTRIPS ARE REPRESENTATIVE OF THE CULTURES OF JAPAN, THE AMERICAN INDIAN, BRAZIL, CENTRAL AFRICA, AND SCANDANAVIA.

FOLKTALES OF ETHNIC AMERICA (P-I-A) THE SIX FILMSTRIPS ARE REPRESENTATIVE OF THE PEOPLE OF AFRICAN, INDIAN, JAPANESE, MEXICAN, PUERTO RICAN, AND ESKIMO HERITAGE.

GETTING TO KNOW ME (P-I-A) EACH OF THESE FOUR FILMSTRIPS RELATES TO UNIVERSAL SITUATIONS AND REACTIONS COMMON AMONG CHILDREN. PORTRAYED ARE CHILDREN OF MULTIETHNIC ORIGIN.

IMMIGRANT FROM AMERICA (A) SHOWS US, A NATION OF IMMIGRANTS, THE INJUSTICE OF RACISM AND THE DEFERENTIAL TREATMENT BETWEEN WHITE IMMIGRANTS AND BLACKS WITHIN THIS COUNTRY THROUGH DENIAL OF OPPORTUNITIES IN EDUCATION, JOBS, CAPITAL, AND POWER.

THE IMPORTANCE OF YOU (P-I-A) FOUR FILMSTRIPS DEPICT SIMILARITIES AND DIFFERENCES AMONG PEOPLE IN DAY-TO-DAY EXPERIENCES COMMON AMONG CHILDREN AND FAMILIES.

LEARNING ABOUT ME (I-A) THESE FIVE FILMSTRIPS PORTRAY MULTIETHNIC GROUPS OF CHILDREN IN TRUE TO LIFE SITUATIONS THAT ARE COMMON AMONG SCHOOL-AGE YOUTH. OPEN ENDED SITUATIONS THAT ENABLE DISCUSSION OF VARIOUS POSSIBLE SOLUTIONS MAKE THESE FILMSTRIPS PARTICULARLY DESIREABLE.

LOLIPOP DRAGON ADVENTURES IN SELF-AWARENESS: THE ME I CAN BE (P-I-A) INCLUDED IN THIS MULTI-MEDIA KIT ARE SIX SOUND FILMSTRIPS, FIFTY ACTIVITY CARDS, FIFTY ACTIVITY SHEETS, A POSTER, CRAYONS, AND A TEACHER'S MANUAL. THE OBJECTIVES ARE SELF WORTH AND THE DIGNITY OF THE INDIVIDUAL AND HUMAN VALUES IN RELATION TO OTHERS. THE LOLIPOP DRAGON'S EXPERIENCES TRANSCEND ETHNIC GROUPS REACHING THE UNIVERSAL ELEMENTS COMMON TO ALL CULTURES AND THE HUMAN DIGNITY OF ALL INDIVIDUALS.

MY HOME AND ME (P-I-A) THESE SIX FILMSTRIPS PRESENT SIX DIFFERENT GEO-GRAPHICAL AREAS OF THE UNITED STATES, THE INFLUENCE OF THE ENVIRONMENT ON PEOPLE, THEIR LIFE-STYLE, WORK, AND RECREATION. REGIONAL ACCENTS AND ENVIRONMENTAL SOUNDS ARE EVIDENCED IN THE RECORDING AND NARRATION AND ADD MUCH TO THE REALISM.

OUR HERITAGE OF AMERICA FOLK MUSIC - SETS I AND II (P-I-A) THE TWELVE FILMSTRIPS OF THIS SERIES PRESENT A HISTORY OF THE CULTURE OF OUR NATION AS THE MUSIC OF EACH HISTORIC PERIOD COMMUNICATES THE EXPERIENCES AND EMOTIONS OF THE PEOPLE OF THAT TIME. THE MUSIC REPRESENTS A CROSS SECTION OF THE ETHNIC GROUPS OF OUR NATION.

PEOPLE ARE HUMAN (I-A) THESE FIVE FILMSTRIPS PROVIDE FOR INTERACTION AS THEY PRESENT SITUATIONS WHICH RELATE TO INTERDEPENDENCY AMONG PEOPLE.

SERENDIPITY BOOKS AND CASSETTES (P-I-A) TWELVE BOOKS, TEN COPIES OF EACH TITLE AND CASSETTES PRESENT STORY CHARACTERS WHICH TRANSCEND ETHNNIC IDENTITY AND PRESENT EXPERIENCES IN HUMAN VALUES THAT ARE UNIVERSAL.

SIX FAMILIES IN THE UNITED STATES (P-I-A) THESE SIX FILMSTRIPS EACH DEPICT THE DAILY LIFE OF A FAMILY OF DIFFERENT ETHNIC, CULTURAL, AND SOCIOECONOMIC BACKGROUND IN VARYING ENVIRONMENTS WITHIN THE UNITED STATES.

SONGSTORIES: I AM SPECIAL AND WHAT MAKES ME THE ONLY ME? (P-I) THESE FOUR FILMSTRIPS OF EACH SET PRESENT UNIVERSAL SITUATIONS THAT ARE COMMON AMONG YOUNG CHILDREN OF VARYING CULTURES AND ETHNIC BACKGROUNDS IN EARLY DEVELOPMENT AND EDUCATIONAL ENVIRONMENT WITH ACCOMPANYING PICTORIAL REPRE-SENTATION OF MULTIETHNIC GROUPS OF CHILDREN.

VALUE SERIES (P-I) THE SERIES IS COMPOSED OF EIGHT SETS OF STUDY PRINTS, EACH SET CONTAINING EIGHT PRINTS PRESENTING PROBLEMS COMMON AMONG CHILDREN AND COVERING THE SCOPE OF ENVIRONMENT AND EXPERIENCE FAMILIAR TO CHILDREN, HOME, FAMILY, NEIGHBORHOOD, SCHOOL, ETC.

WILLIAM, ANDY, AND RAMON AND FIVE FRIENDS AT SCHOOL (P-I) THESE SIX FILMSTRIPS PRESENT EXPERIENCES AMONG BOYS OF DIFFERENT ETHNIC AND CULTURAL BACKGROUNDS WHO ARE LIVING IN THE SAME URBAN COMMUNITY.

CHICANO AMERICAN FILMS AND FILMSTRIPS

ALA BRAVA: PRISON AND BEYOND/THE BLACK PEARL (1973) 54 MINS. B/W (I-A)
THIS TWO PART FILMSTRIP IS BASED ON THE BOOK OF THE SAME TITLE BY SCOTT
O'DELL AND IS THE STORY OF RAMON, A PEARL DIVER ON THE COAST OF BAJA,
CALIFORNIA.

CENTRAL AMERICA AND THE CARIBBEAN (I-A) THESE SIX FILMSTRIPS PRESENT THE
VARIED PATTERNS OF LIVING AMONG THE PEOPLE OF ADJACENT COMMUNITIES IN
CENTRAL AMERICA: COSTA RICA, GUATAMALA, PUERTO RICO, CUBA, AND THE ISLANDS
OF THE CARIBBEAN.

CHICANO (1972) 23 MINS. (I-A) FILMED AT A POLITICAL PROTEST RALLY IN
EAST LOS ANGELES, THE MEXICAN AMERICANS TELL OF THE DISCRIMINATION THROUGH-
OUT THE BARRIO AND WHAT THEY SHOULD HAVE IN ORDER TO BE EQUAL TO OTHER ANGLO
AREAS. THE EDUCATION SYSTEM EXCLUDES THEM AS A PEOPLE AND IS DESIGNED FOR
A MONO-LINGUAL LEARNING SITUATION. IT ALSO PRESENTS THE GOALS OF THE
CHICANO MOVEMENT.

CUBA AND ITS REFUGEES (I-A) TWO FILMSTRIPS WHICH PRESENT THE HISTORY,
ECONOMY, POLITICS, AND CULTURE OF CUBA AND THE IMPACT OF THE CUBAN REFUGEES
ON THE UNITED STATES.

FAMILIES OF MEXICO AND CENTRAL AMERICA (I-A) THESE FOUR FILMSTRIPS SURVEY
THE FAMILY STRUCTURE AND LIFESTYLE AMONG THE PEOPLE OF DIFFERENT SOCIO-
ECONOMIC ENVIRONMENTS FROM HONDURAS, GUATAMALA, YUCATAN, AND MEXICO.

FAMILIES OF SOUTH AMERICA (I-A) THESE FOUR FILMSTRIPS EXPLORE FAMILY
PATTERNS AMONG DIFFERENT ENVIRONMENTS IN SOUTH AMERICA AND THE INFLUENCE OF
CULTURAL SIMILARITIES AND DIFFERENCES.

FAMILIES OF SOUTH AMERICA (P-I) THESE SIX FILMSTRIPS PRESENT THE FIVERSE
CULTURES AND LIFESTYLES REFLECTING GEOGRAPHIC AND ECONOMIC INFLUENCE OF AND
ON THE CONTINENT OF SOUTH AMERICA.

FOLKTALES OF LATIN AMERICA (P-I) THE SIX FILMSTRIPS OF THIS SERIES
PRESENT FOLKTALES FROM MEXICO AND PUERTO RICO RELATING TRADITIONS AND
CULTURE COMMON AMONG THE LATIN AMERICAN PEOPLE.

FOLKTALES OF SOUTH AMERICA (P-I) THE SIX FILMSTRIPS OF THIS SERIES ARE
REPRESENTATIVE OF THE VARIED CULTURES OF THE PEOPLE OF DIFFERENT COUNTRIES
IN SOUTH AMERICA WITH SPECIAL ATTENTION TO AUTHENTIC PORTRAYAL OF CUSTOMS
AND DRESS.

FOUR BOYS OF CENTRAL AMERICA   (I-A)   EACH OF THESE FOUR FILMSTRIPS PORTRAY THE LIFE OF PEOPLE IN DIFFERENT SOCIOECONOMIC ENVIRONMENTS: THE CITY, A BANANA PLANTATION, A FISHING VILLAGE, AND AN INDIAN VILLAGE. THE IMPORTANCE OF FAMILY TRADITIONS AND EXPECTATIONS ARE EVIDENCED IN EACH.

I AM JOAQUIN (1971) 20 MINS. (I-A)   THE EVOLUTION OF THE MEXICAN AMERICAN CULTURE FROM THE MAYAN PRINCES TO THE CHICANO MOVEMENT. TODAY'S RESULTS OF PAST INEQUITIES CHANGED THEIR VALUES AND THIS FILM ATTEMPTS TO SHOW THE CON-TEMPORARY CHICANO'S SEARCH FOR IDENTITY.

MEXICO I (P-I-A) AMONG THE TWENTY-FOUR PRINTS OF THIS SET ARE THOSE DEPICTING THE CITIES, THE COUNTRYSIDE, CRAFTS, ART, ARCHITECTURE, INDUSTRIES, AND PEOPLE OF MEXICO. THE PICTURE STORY STUDY PRINTS PROVIDE RESOURCE MATERIAL AND PERTINENT INFORMATION ABOUT THE COUNTRY.

SOUTH AMERICA TODAY (P-I-A) AMONG THE FORTY-EIGHT INDIVIDUAL PICTURE STORY STUDY PRINTS OF THIS SET ARE REPRESENTATIVE LIFE AND CULTURE STUDIES OF ALL OF THE COUNTRIES OF SOUTH AMERICA.

SPANISH AMERICAN LEADERS OF THE 20TH CENTURY IN AMERICA (P-I-A) THESE EIGHT FILMSTRIPS PRESENT BIOGRAPHIES OF FOUR MEXICAN AMERICANS AND FOUR PUERTO RICANS WHO HAVE OVERCOME ADVERSITIES TO BECOME OUTSTANDING PERSONS AMONG THEIR OWN ETHNIC GROUPS AND CONTRIBUTORS TO THE HERITAGE OF OUR NATION.

BLACK AMERICAN FILMS AND FILMSTRIPS

ACROSS FIVE APRILS (P-I) THIS SET OF TWO FILMSTRIPS PRESENTS THE STORY BASED ON THE BOOK BY IRENE HUNT.

AFRICA: CONTINENT IN CHANGE (I-A) A SET OF FIVE FILMSTRIPS PRESENTING THE TRADITIONS AND CULTURES OF THE DIVERSIFIED PEOPLE OF AFRICA IN THIS PERIOD OF RAPID CHANGE IN EMERGING AND DEVELOPING NATIONS.

AFRICA: FOCUS ON CULTURE (I-A) THIS SET OF FOUR FILMSTRIPS PRESENT THE TRADITIONAL NATIVE CULTURES AND TRANSITIONS WHICH ARE OCCURRING IN THE CONTEMPORARY LIFE OF THESE PEOPLE.

AFRICAN FOLK LEGENDS (P-I-A) THIS SET OF SIX FILMSTRIPS PRESENTS LEGENDS FROM THE HERITAGE OF AFRICA, EACH OF WHICH IS QUITE SIMILAR TO AESOP'S FABLES IN THAT THERE IS A PERTINENT MORAL WHICH REINFORCES THE UNIVERSAL SIMILARITIES SHARED AMONG THE CULTURES OF THE WORLD.

AFRICAN FOLKTALES (P-I-A) A SET OF SIX FILMSTRIPS WHICH RELATES LEGENDS AND FABLES OF AFRICAN STORYTELLERS WHICH BRING BOTH HISTORY AND CULTURE TO THE VIEWER-LISTENER.

AFRICAN FOLKTALES (P-I-A) THIS SET OF SIX FILMSTRIPS PRESENTS NATIVE FOLKTALES OF THE CULTURES AND VALUES INHERENT AMONG THE PEOPLE WHO HAVE PERPETUATED THE RETELLING OF THESE STORIES FOR GENERATIONS.

AMERICAN NEGROES (P-I) A SET OF EIGHT CAPTIONED FILMSTRIPS, EACH PRE-SENTING THE BIOGRAPHY OF A FAMOUS BLACK MAN OR WOMAN AND THE CONTRIBUTION THAT PERSON'S ENDEAVORS MADE TO THE HERITAGE OF THE BLACK AMERICAN AND THE HISTORY OF THIS NATION.

AMERICAN NEGRO PATHFINDERS (I-A) A SET OF SIX FILMSTRIPS WHICH RELATE THE NOTED CONTRIBUTIONS TO SOCIETY FOR THE CAUSES OF INDIVIDUAL FREEDOM, HUMAN DIGNITY, AND SOCIAL JUSTICE.

AMOS FORTUNE, FREE MAN (I) THIS SET OF TWO FILMSTRIPS PRESENTS THE STORY WHICH IS BASED ON THE BOOK BY ELIZABETH YATES.

ANASI THE SPIDER (P-I-A) A FILMSTRIP WHICH PRESENTS A FOLKTALE FROM THE BOOK OF THE SAME NAME WHICH WAS WRITTEN BY GERALD MCDERMOTT AND PUBLISHED BY HOLT, RHINEHART, AND WINSTON. THE FILMSTRIP HAS EXCELLENT PICTURES AND A MOST EFFECTIVE NARRATION.

BLACK LEADERS OF 20TH CENTURY AMERICA (I-A) A SET OF TEN FILMSTRIPS, EACH TELLING THE STORY OF A LEADING BLACK MAN OR WOMAN OF THIS CENTURY WHO HAS BEEN AN OUTSTANDING LEADER IN THE ARTS, SCIENCE, OR POLITICS.

CHAINS OF SLAVERY (1800 - 1865) (A) A SET OF SIX TITLES IN FILMSTRIP FORMAT WHICH IS ACCOMPANIED BY A TEXTBOOK. THE SET IS DETAILED, EXPLICIT, AND A FIRM BASIS FOR UNDERSTANDING SLAVERY AND WHAT IT REALLY MEANS.

THE DREAM AWAKE (I-A) SEVEN FILMSTRIPS AND THIRTY-THREE STUDY PRINTS PRESENT A PROGRAM OF THE BLACK EXPERIENCE IN AMERICA FROM THE FIRST DAYS OF SLAVERY THROUGHOUT HISTORY TO THE PRESENT TIME.

FAMILIES OF EAST AFRICA/FAMILIES OF WEST AFRICA: LIFE IN THE CITY/FAMILIES OF WEST AFRICA: FARMERS AND FISHERMEN (P-I-A) EACH OF THE THREE TITLES WITHIN THE UNIT HAS FOUR FILMSTRIPS WHICH PRESENT DIVERSITY AMONG FAMILIES BASED ON GEOGRAPHY, ECONOMY, CULTURE, AND CONTEMPORARY SOCIETY.

FAMILIES OF MODERN BLACK AFRICA (P-I) THREE FILMSTRIPS, EACH ONE A VISIT WITH A FAMILY IN AFRICA IN THE SETTING OF A VILLAGE, A CITY, AND AN INDUSTRIAL COMMUNITY.

LEADING AMERICAN NEGROES (I) THESE SIX FILMSTRIPS EACH PRESENT A BIOGRAPHY OF AN OUTSTANDING MAN OR WOMAN OF BLACK HERITAGE AND THE CONTRIBUTIONS EACH MADE TOWARD IMPROVING CONDITIONS FOR THE BLACK PEOPLE AND OUR NATION AS A WHOLE.

PEARL PRIMUS' AFRICA: FOLKTALES OF OMOWALE (P-I) THIS IS A SET OF THREE CASSETTES WITH MS. PRIMUS' STORYTELLING ABILITY LENDING A MOVING BEAUTY TO THE MANY FOLKTALES AND PROVERBS RELATED FROM THE CULTURAL HERITAGE OF AFRICA.

A PEOPLE UPROOTED (1500 - 1800) (I-A) A SET OF SEVEN TITLES IN FILMSTRIP FORMAT TOGETHER WITH TEN TEXTBOOKS.

QUEST FOR EQUALITY (1910 TO PRESENT) (I-A) THE SETS OF FILMSTRIPS, TEXTS, AND DISCS PRESENT AN INTERRELATED MULTI-MEDIA PROGRAM OF BLACK PARTICIPATION IN AMERICAN HISTORY WITH SPECIFIC ATTENTION GIVEN TO PEOPLE, PLACES, AND EVENTS IN THE DEVELOPMENT OF THIS COUNTRY.

ROBERT AND HIS FAMILY (P) FOUR FILMSTRIPS WHICH PRESENT A BLACK BOY AND HIS FAMILY IN AN URBAN SETTING: HIS HOME, SCHOOL, NEIGHBORHOOD, AND COMMUNITY.

SEPARATE AND UNEQUAL (1865 - 1910) (P-I-A) SET OF SIX TITLES IN FILMSTRIP
FORMAT ACCOMPANIED BY A SET OF TEN TEXTBOOKS. VERY EFFECTIVE UNIT.

A SOCIAL HISTORY OF BLACK AMERICANS (I-A) THIS SET OF SIX FILMSTRIPS PRE-
SENT A DOCUMENTARY RECORD OF LIFE IN BLACK AMERICA WHICH COVERS THE TIME
FROM SLAVERY TO CONTEMPORARY TIME.

A STORY - A STORY (I-A) THIS FILMSTRIP PRESENTS A FOLKTALE BASED ON THE
BOOK OF THE SAME TITLE BY GALE E. HALEY AND PUBLISHED BY ATHENEUM PRESS.
IT'S A VERY EFFECTIVE STRIP WITH OUTSTANDING NARRATION.

WHAT MARY JO SHARED / WHAT MARY JO WANTED (P-I) THIS SET OF TWO FILM-
STRIPS PRESENT TWO EVENT OF DAILY LIFE OF A BLACK AMERICAN CHILD, MARY JO,
IN CONTEMPORARY LIFE. THESE TWO EVENTS ARE UNIVERSALLY SHARED AND ALSO
"SHAREABLE" EXPERIENCES AND EMOTIONS AMONG YOUNG CHILDREN. THE UNIT IS
BASED ON LITERATURE BY J. M. UDRY AND PUBLISHED BY A. WHITMAN AND COMPANY.

ASIAN AMERICAN FILMS AND FILMSTRIPS

ASIAN FOLKTALES (P-I) SIX FILMSTRIPS DEPICTING THE FOLKTALES OF SIX DIFFERENT AREAS, EACH AREA OR CULTURE ACCOMPANIED BY ILLUSTRATIONS, AUTHENTIC MUSIC, AND QUALITY NARRATION.

AUSTRALIA AND NEW ZEALAND (I-A) THESE SIX FILMSTRIPS PORTRAY LIFE AMONG THE POLYNESIANS, MAORIS, AND PEOPLE OF EUROPEAN AND BRITISH BACKGROUNDS SHARING IN THE DEVELOPMENT OF THEIR RESPECTIVE COUNTRIES AND AREAS IN AUSTRALIA AND NEW ZEALAND.

CHINA TODAY (I-A) THESE SIX FILMSTRIPS TELL OF CHINA'S FOUR THOUSAND YEAR HISTORY, OF THE CULTURAL REVOLUTION, AND OF THE COMMUNES OF CONTEMPORARY CHINA. THE CHANGES IN THE TRADITIONAL WAY OF LIFESTYLE THROUGH THE INFLUENCE OF THE PEOPLE'S REPUBLIC ARE ILLUSTRATED.

FAMILIES OF ASIA (P-I-A) THESE SIX FILMSTRIPS ILLUSTRATE SIMILARITIES AND DIFFERENCES AMONG FAMILY LIFE IN HONG KONG, BANGLADESH, INDIA, JAPAN, JAVA, AND THAILAND.

FAMILIES OF SOUTHEAST ASIA (P-I-A) THESE FOUR FILMSTRIPS ILLUSTRATE THE WAY OF LIFE, CULTURE, HISTORY, AND GENERAL ACTIVITIES OF THE PEOPLES OF INDONESIA, MALAYSIA, SINGAPORE, AND THE PHILIPPINES.

FAMILIES OF SOUTHWEST ASIA (P-I-A) THESE FOUR FILMSTRIPS ILLUSTRATE FAMILY LIFE, ECONOMY, HISTORY, AND SOME OF THE CULTURE OF THE PEOPLES OF EGYPT, IRAN, TURKEY, AND LEBANON.

FOLKTALES OF CHINA (P-I-A) EACH OF THE SIX FILMSTRIPS PORTRAYS FOLKTALES IN A WORK OF ART NARRATED BY HANS CONREID. THE AUTHENTIC TALES EVIDENCE THE CULTURE AND VALUES OF THE CHINESE HERITAGE.

FOUR FAMILIES OF JAPAN (I-A) FOUR FILMSTRIPS PRESENT SIMILARITIES AND CONTRASTS AMONG FAMILIES OF DIVERSE SOCIOECONOMIC SETTINGS IN CONTEMPORARY JAPAN, REFLECTING CULTURE AND THE TRADITION BORN OF LONG HISTORY.

JAPAN - LAND OF THE KAMI (A) SURVEY OF MODERN JAPANESE RELIGIONS WHICH HAVE EVOLVED FROM THE TRADITIONAL SHINTO AND BHUDDIST RELIGIONS. THE BASIC RELIGIOSITY OF THE JAPANESE PEOPLE IS ILLUSTRATED THROUGH RITUALS, DRESS, AND THEIR EVERYDAY APPROACH TO LIFE.

JAPAN: SPIRIT OF IEMOTO (P-I) IN THESE FIVE FILMSTRIPS, THE CULTURE AND TRADITION EMBODIED IN THE SYSTEM OF FAMILY RELATIONSHIPS, RESPECT, RELIGION, AND LOVE OF NATURE ARE RELATED THROUGH THE LIFESTYLE OF PEOPLE IN JAPAN, NOW.

THE NEW JAPAN (I-A) SIX FILMSTRIPS ILLUSTRATE THE NEW JAPAN WITH SPECIAL EMPHASIS ON THE DIVERSITY IN INDUSTRY, PATTERNS OF LIFE, AND THE INFLUENCE OF TRADITIONS AND CUSTOMS AMONG THE PEOPLE.

ORIENTAL BICULTURE MINI LIBRARY (I-A) SIX SOUND FILMSTRIPS OF THE NOTABLE BOOKS, THE HOUSE OF SIXTY FATHERS, BY MEINDERT DEJONG, SHEN OF THE SEA, BY ARTHUR B. CHRISMAN, YOUNG FU OF THE UPPER YANGTZE, BY ELIZABETH F. LEWIS, AND THE CAT THAT WENT TO HEAVEN, BY ELIZABETH COATSWORTH. A CASSETTE RECORDING OF DRAGON WINGS, BY LAWRENCE YEP IS INCLUDED IN THE SERIES.

SOUTHEAST ASIA: PAST AND PRESENT (I-A) TWO FILMSTRIPS PORTRAY THE WAY OF LIFE AMONG THE PEOPLES OF CAMBODIA, MALAYSIA, THAILAND, AND VIETNAM.

TAIWAN (I-A) THESE TWO FILMSTRIPS PRESENT THE PLANS OF AN EMERGING COUNTRY, ITS INDUSTRY, RURAL LIFE, CULTURE, AND CHANGING LIFE STYLE. THIS UNIT IS PARTICULARLY INTERESTING IN LIGHT OF OUR REAPPROACHMENT OF CHINA ..... THE PEOPLE'S REPUBLIC.

NATIVE AMERICAN FILMS AND FILMSTRIPS

AMERICAN INDIAN FOLK LEGENDS (P-I-A) SIX FILMSTRIPS, EACH THE RETELLING OF AN INDIAN LEGEND OF THE WAYS OF ANIMALS IN NATURE, WITH A VALUABLE LESSON IN HUMAN VALUES.

AMERICAN INDIAN LEGENDS (P-I-A) THESE SIX FILMSTRIPS REPRESENT CULTURAL AND TRADITIONAL BELIEFS OF SIX INDIAN TRIBES: CHEROKEE, SEMINOLE, KIOWA, HAIDA, CHOCTAW, AND ESKIMO.

AMERICAN INDIAN LEGENDS (P-I-A) THESE FOUR FILMSTRIPS ILLUSTRATE THE LEGENDS RELATING TO THE UNITY OF LIFE WITH NATURE AND TRIBAL COHESIVE RELATIONS. REPRESENTED ARE THE: IROQUOIS, CHEROKEE, UTE, AND MESCALERO APACHE. THE ART, MUSIC, AND NARRATION ARE EXCELLENT.

AMERICAN INDIAN TALES FOR CHILDREN (P-I) TWO CASSETTES FEATURING INDIAN TALES OF ANIMALS AND THE SPIRIT OF NATURE.

ARROW TO THE SUN (I-A) A PUEBLO INDIAN LEGEND BASED ON A BOOK BY THE SAME TITLE BY GERALD MCDERMOTT, PUBLISHED BY VIKING PRESS. ART AND NARRATION ARE EXCELLENT.

BROKEN TREATY AT BATTLE MOUNTAIN (1975) 58 MINS. COLOR (I-A) SHOSHONE INDIANS STRUGGLE TO REGAIN THEIR ANCESTRAL LANDS AND EXCLUDE ITS USE BY HUNTERS AND FISHERMEN. THE GOVERNMENT WANTS THEM TO SELL THEIR LAND AND SOME MEMBERS OF THE TRIBE WANT TO SELL WHILE OTHERS WANT TO RETAIN THEIR HERITAGE AND RITUALS BY KEEPING THEIR LAND AND MAINTAINING TRIBAL INTEGRITY.

END OF THE TRAIL (1966) 54MINS. B/W (I-A) WALTER BRENNAN NARRATES A HISTORY OF THE PLAINS INDIANS FOLLOWING THE CIVIL WAR FOLLOWING THEIR DEMISE AS A NATION, AND CIVILIZATION. THE FILM CON-CLUDES WITH CUSTER'S DEFEAT AS TOLD BY THE SURVIVORS. THE FILM DEPICTS THE WAY OF LIFE AND THE LAWS WHICH FORCED CHANGE ON THE INDIANS AND THEIR RETALLIATION. HERE IS AN EXCELLENT HISTORICAL FILM AND ONE WHICH HAS A BRILLIANT TECHNICAL PRODUCTION TO BACK IT.

THE FIRST AMERICANS (I-A) THESE SIX FILMSTRIPS PRESENT THE CUSTOMS AND CULTURE OF THE INDIAN TRIBES OF THE NORTHEAST, SOUTHWEST, GREAT LAKES, PLAINS, SOUTHEAST, AND NORTHWEST. THE STRUGGLE TO RETAIN THE CIVILIZATION INHERENT WITHIN EACH UNIQUE TRIBE IS EVIDENCED IN THE HISTORICAL DEVELOP-MENTS PORTRAYED.

FOLKTALES OF NORTH AMERICAN INDIANS (P-I-A) EACH OF THE SIX FILMSTRIPS DEPICTS A FOLKTALE FROM A DIFFERENT TRIBE, WITH THE UNIVERSAL THEME OF THE INFLUENCE OF NATURE.

GREAT AMERICAN INDIAN HEROES (I-A) EACH OF THE EIGHT FILMSTRIPS WITHIN THIS SERIES PRESENTS A PERSONAL STORY OF A LEADER OF AN INDIAN TRIBE. THE BIOGRAPHIES ARE OF: TECUMSEH, OSCEOLA, BLACK HAWK, PONTIAC, CHIEF JOSEPH, SITTING BULL, GERONIMO, AND JOSEPH BRANT.

INDIANS OF NORTH AMERICA (I-A) THESE FIVE FILMSTRIPS TRACE THE HISTORY OF CULTURE, CEREMONY, AND CONFLICT TOGETHER WITH THE CHANGING LIFE PATTERNS FOR THE NATIVE AMERICANS FROM EARLY HISTORY TO THE PRESENT DAY.

INDIANS OF NORTH AMERICA (I-A) THESE SIX FILMSTRIPS PORTRAY THE ECONOMIC, SOCIAL, AND SPIRITUAL ASPECTS OF TRIBAL LIFE RELATIVE TO THE CULTURE AND GEOGRAPHIC ENVIRONMENT OF EACH TRIBE.

INDIANS OF THE UNITED STATES AND CANADA (I-A) THE FORTY-EIGHT PRINTS RELATE THE WORK, CULTURE, CRAFTS, AND LIFESTYLE OF A REPRESENTATION OF THE INDIANS OF NORTH AMERICA. INFORMATION AND RESOURCES ARE INCLUDED WITH EACH STUDY PRINT.

LEGENDS FROM THE LAND OF SUN AND SNOW (P-I-A) THESE FOUR FILMSTRIPS PROVIDE TWO LEGENDS FROM THE HOPI INDIANS OF THE SOUTHWEST AND TWO FROM THE ESKIMO INDIANS OF THE FAR NORTH; ALL RELATING VALUES, GOALS, DESIRES, AND VIEWS OF THE HUMAN CONDITION.

THE LIFE OF THE AMERICAN INDIAN (P-I-A) THESE TWO FILMSTRIPS COVER THE CULTURE, CUSTOMS, CONFLICT, AND TRADITIONS OF THE EAST WOODLANDS, THE PLAINS, THE NORTHWEST COAST, AND THE SOUTHWEST INDIANS.

NATIVE AMERICAN HERITAGE (I-A) FIVE FILMSTRIPS USE ART AND PHOTOGRAPHY TO TRACE THE NATIVE AMERICAN CULTURE FROM COLONIAL DAYS TO THE PRESENT.

NAVAJO FOLKLORE (P-I-A) THESE FOUR FILMSTRIPS DEPICT THE ESSENCE OF NAVAJO FOLKLORE, VITAL TO THE EDUCATION AND CULTURE OF THE PEOPLE AND THEIR WAY OF LIFE AND THE SIGNIFICANCE OF NATURE INHERENT IN THEIR BELIEFS.

SIX NATIVE AMERICAN FAMILIES (P-I-A) THESE SIX FILMSTRIPS DEPICT THE FAMILY LIFE OF THE: SIOUX, MOHAWK, SEMINOLE, NAVAJO, PUEBLO, AND KAWKIUTL. VERY AUTHENTIC, UTLIZING A FAMILY MEMBER AS NARRATOR OF EACH FILM WITH EXCELLENT DEPICTION OF LIFE, WORK, TRADITION AND CULTURAL INVOLVMENT.

WILDERNESS KINGDOM (I-A) FOUR FILMSTRIPS WHICH PRESENT A DOCUMENTARY OF THE LIFE OF ROCKY MOUNTAIN AND PLAINS INDIANS, BASED ON THE PAINTINGS AND DIARIES OF FATHER NICHOLAS POINT, A PIONEER FRENCH MISSIONARY WHO LIVED AMONG THESE PEOPLE FROM 1840 TO 1847.

THE AUTHORS WISH TO ACKNOWLEDGE THE HELP OF ROBERT GASTON AND PATRICIA HARP, BOTH DOCTORAL CANDIDATES AT THE UNIVERSITY OF NEVADA.LAS VEGAS, IN THE PREPARATION OF THIS LISTING.

SUGGESTED READING LIST FOR CHILDREN

CHICANO AMERICAN

ACUNA, RUDY. CULTURES IN CONFLICT. CHARTER SCHOOL BOOKS, 1970.

-----. THE STORY OF THE MEXICAN AMERICANS. AMERICAN BOOK COMPANY, 1969.

ATWATER, JAMES D. AND RAMON E. RUIZ. OUT FROM UNDER. DOUBLEDAY, 1969.

BAYLOR, BOYD. COYOTE CRY. LOTHROP, LEE, AND SHEPARD COMPANY, 1972.

COATSWORTH, ELIZABETH. THE PLACE. HOLT, RHINEHART, AND WINSTON, 1966.

DARBOIS, DOMINIQUE. TACHO, BOY OF MEXICO. FOLLETT, 1961.

ETS, MARIE HALL. GIBERTO AND THE WIND. VIKING PRESS, 1963.

FITCH, ROBERT AND OYNN. SOY CHICANO: I AM A MEXICAN AMERICAN. CREATIVE
    EDUCATIONAL SOCIETY, 1970.

FRANCHERE, RUTH. CESAR CHAVEZ. CORWELL, 1970.

MARTIN, PATRICIA. CHICANOS. PARENTS MAGAZINE PRESS, 1971.

-----. CHICANOS: MEXICANS IN THE UNITED STATES. PARENTS MAGAZINE PRESS,
    1971.

MOLNAR, JOE. GRACIELA: A MEXICAN AMERICAN CHILD TELLS HER STORY.
    FRANKLIN WATTS, 1972.

NAVA, JULIAN. MEXICAN AMERICANS, A BRIEF LOOK AT THEIR HISTORY. ANTI-
    DEFAMATION LEAGUE OF B'NAI B'RITH, 1970.

-----. MEXICAN AMERICANS, PAST, PRESENT, AND FUTURE. AMERICAN BOOK COMPANY,
    1969.

NEWLON, CLARKE. FAMOUS MEXICAN AMERICANS. DODD, MEAD, AND COMPANY, 1972.

O'CONNELL, JAMES. LOS PRIMEROS. FOLLETT, 1969.

POLITO, LEO. PEDRO, THE ANGEL OF OLIVERA STREET. CHARLES SCRIBNER AND
    SONS, 1946.

-----. JUANITA. CHARLES SCRIBNER AND SONS, 1948.

-----. ROSA. CHARLES SCRIBNER AND SOSN, 1963.

PRIETO, MARIANA. A KITE FOR CARLOS. JOHN DAY COMPANY, 1966.

RITCHIE, BARBRA. RAMON MAKES A TRADE. HALE AND COMPANY, 1964.

ROSS, PATRICIA. <u>MEXICO</u>. FIEDLER COMPANY, 1971.

TEBBEL, JOHN AND RAMON E. RUIZ. <u>SOUTH BY SOUTHWEST: THE MEXICAN AMERICAN
     AND HIS HERITAGE</u>. DOUBLEDAY, 1969.

WEINER, SANDRA. <u>SMALL HANDS, BIG HANDS: SEVEN PROFILES OF CHICANO MIGRANT
     WORKERS AND THEIR FAMILIES</u>. PANTHEON BOOKS, 1970.

BLACK AMERICAN

ADAMS, RUSSEL L. GREATE NEGROES PAST AND PRESENT. AFRO-AMERICAN PRESS, 1969.

ADOFF, ARNOLD. BLACK IS BROWN IS TAN. HARPER AND ROW, 1973.

-----, ED. THE POETRY OF BLACK AMERICA: ANTHOLOGY OF THE 20TH CENTURY. HARPER AND ROW, 1973.

ANDERSON, MARIAN. MY LORD, WHAT A MORNING. VIKING PRESS, 1955.

ARMSTRONG, WILLIAM H. SOUNDER. HARPER AND ROW, 1972.

BANKS, JAMES A. AND CHEERY A. MARCH TOWARD FREEDOM: A HISTORY OF BLACK AMERICANS. FEARON BOOKS, 1974.

BERNARD, JACQUELINE. JOURNEY TOWARD FREEDOM: THE STORY OF SOJOURNER TRUTH. NORTON, 1967.

BONHAM, FRANK. DURANGO STREET. DUTTON, 1965.

BONTEMPS, ARNA. FREDERICK DOUGLASS. ALFRED A. KNOPF, 1959.

-----. STORY OF THE NEGRO. ALFRED A. KNOPF, 1948.

BRAITHWAITE, E.R. TO SIR, WITH LOVE. PYRAMID BOOKS, 1968.

BROOKS, GWENDOLYN. BRONZEVILLE BOYS AND GIRLS. HARPER AND ROW, 1956.

BRYAN, ASHLEY. THE OX OF THE WONDERFUL HORNS AND OTHER AFRICAN FOLKTALES. ANTHENEUM, 1971.

CARLSON, NATALIE SAVAGE. THE EMPTY SCHOOLHOUSE. HARPER, 1965.

CARRUTH, ELLA KAISER. SHE WANTED TO READ: THE STORY OF MARY MCLEOD BETHUME. ABINGDON BOOKS, 1966.

CHITTENDON, ELIZABETH F. PROFILES IN BLACK AND WHITE: STORIES OF MEN AND WOMEN WHO FOUGHT AGAINST SLAVERY. CHARLES SCRIBNER AND SONS, 1973.

CLAYTON, EDWARD C. MARTIN LUTHER KING: PEACEFUL WARRIOR. PRENTICE-HALL, 1965.

CLIFTON, LUCILLE. ALL US CROSS THE WATER. HOLT, RHINEHART, 1973.

-----. THE BLACK BC'S. DUTTON PUBLISHING COMPANY, 1970.